FLAVORS of VAIL

Peak Properties

Vail, Colorado
www.peakpropertiesvail.com

Flavors of Vail

Published by Peak Properties

    1000 Lions Ridge Loop, Suite 3A, Vail, Colorado 81657

    E-mail: info@peakpropertiesvail.com   Website: www.peakpropertiesvail.com

Commissioning Editor: Carolyn Dielmann Connolly

10 9 8 7 6 5 4 3 2 1

Printed in Canada.

Callawind
Custom Cookbooks

Produced by Callawind Custom Cookbooks
A division of Callawind Publications Inc.

3539 St. Charles Boulevard, Suite 179, Kirkland, Quebec, Canada H9H 3C4
2083 Hempstead Turnpike, PMB 355, East Meadow, New York, USA 11554-1711
E-mail: info@callawind.com   Website: www.callawind.com

Design: Marcy Claman
Indexing: Heather Ebbs

Table of Contents

PAUL FERZACCA, LA TOUR RESTAURANT, 35

Escargot in Sauce Persillé (French Helix Snails Cooked in Parsley Sauce), 37

Field Green Salad with Toasted Goat Cheese, Dried Cranberry, Pine Nuts,
Whole Grain Mustard Vinaigrette, 38

Dover Sole Meunière with Haricots Vert, Baby Creamer Potatoes,
Lemon Brown Butter Sauce, 40

Crème Brûlèe Flambé with Grand Marnier Macerated Berries, 42

THOMAS SALAMUNOVICH, LARKSPUR RESTAURANT, 43

Colorado Organic Tomato Tower with House-Made Mozzarella and Basil, 45

Butternut Squash Soup with Pumpkin Seed Oil, Fried Sage and Beet Powder, 46

Oven Roasted Liberty Duck with Root Vegetable Stuffing and Cranberry Relish, 48

American Apple Pie with Vanilla Bean Ice Cream and Concord Grape Sauce, 50

Iranian and Trout Caviars with Crème Fraîche and Chervil-Potato Blinis, 52

DANIEL JOLY, MIRABELLE AT BEAVER CREEK, 53

Vegetable Ravioli with Asparagus Coulis, 54

Dover Sole Meunière, 55

Grilled Lobster Fricassee with Garlic Sauce, 56

Warm Crêpes with Golden Apples, 57

PINEY RIVER RANCH, 58

Piney River Ranch Cheesy Artichoke Dip, 60

Grilled Portobello Mushroom Sandwich with Goat Cheese and Tangy Mayonnaise, 61

Kevin Nelson, Terra Bistro, 62

Ice Cold Gazpacho with Dungeness Crab Salad and Crème Fraîche, 63

California Sea Bass with Lemon and Basil in Tomato Consommé, Served with a Smoked Salmon Risotto Cake and Garnished with Parsley Relish, 64

Venison Loin with Caramelized Onion Ratatouille, Sundried Tomato Demi-Glace, and Gorgonzola Gratinée, 66

White Bean and Squash Sauté, 68

INTERNATIONAL FLAVORS

Appetizers, 71

Tchouchoukka, 71

Shrimp Salsa Dip, 72

Soups, 73

Blue Cheese Vichyssoise, 73

Spicy Garbanzo Bean and Chicken Sausage Soup, 74

Gulyás Soup (Gulyásleves), 75

Salads, 76

Smoked Salmon Pasta Salad, 76

Summer Cucumber Salad, 77

Cornbread Salad, 78

CHEF

Flavors

Rutherford Maule

CHEF DE MAISON

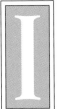have worked my way around several of the world's leading kitchens throughout my 16-year career as a chef. I spent several years in Europe with acclaimed restaurants, including the Hotel Savoy-London, the Hotel Savoie-France, and then several years at Australian icon restaurants, where my interest in Asian/French fusion was kindled. I began my career at Petite Lyon-New Zealand where I completed a four-year in apprenticeship with several of New Zealand's leading chefs in the country's most awarded restaurant. I now live in Vail full-time, and am the owner and chef de cuisine of Chef de Maison catering and personal chef services.

Chef de Maison is a full service high-end catering and personal chef company in Vail. During the winter I spend many dining times with families from all over the country and world as they vacation here in Vail. It's a complete service: prior to arrival we establish any dietary requirements or preferences, a menu is drawn up and ingredients ordered from purveyors around the country. My emphasis is on fantastic fresh produce using farm-raised and organic as much as possible. Shelves are stocked with groceries for the clients' stay, with prepared meals in the refrigerator and a chef dressed in full whites ready to cook to the special requests of the family, group of friends or corporate group. Coming into a client's house as a personal chef means preparing the meals in front of them; it can often turn into a cooking lesson. I spend a lot of time around the clients in one of the most social places in the house — I often feel like one of the group by the time their vacation ends!

The catering aspect of the business is diverse. I cover the range from five-course sit-down dinners to cocktail parties, from formal banquets to casual family get-togethers. I take pride in personally tailoring the menus to meet the desires of the host as well as any guests' specific requirements. I am often asked 'why not open a restaurant?' The answer is simple: I enjoy the flexibility of serving a different menu every day, in a different kitchen,

Chef de Maison

PREMIUM CATERING & PERSONAL CHEF SERVICES

surrounded by a new group of people. It keeps things interesting while I do the thing I love to do: cooking up a storm!

Growing up in New Zealand, the kitchen was the family hub. We would all get involved with helping mum with family dinners, making soups, preserving fruits, helping prepare and serve dinner parties. The food could be really simple but the emphasis was on the enjoyment of making it and the delight in eating it; they both went hand-in-hand. Thus grew my appreciation for food. I think it is imperative for a chef of any level to cook with a large helping of passion. The journey through the kitchen should be pleasurable as it is a temporary art, largely savored in memory.

I hope that these recipes will act as a tool for experimentation, as they hold the formulas of the evolution of this chef. Each chef or cook develops as an individual as he or she accumulates a repertoire shaped by encounters with other chefs, in journeys from kitchen to kitchen and around the globe.

Bon appetit!

Rutherford Maule, Chef de Maison

Coconut Yellowtail and Gulf Shrimp Ceviche

Chef de Maison

This recipe can either serve 6 as a starter or 12 in a shot glass for an appetizer.

½ pound fresh gulf shrimp (can substitute any fresh jumbo shrimp)

⅓ pound fresh yellowtail (can substitute tuna, salmon, halibut or swordfish)

2 cups light coconut milk

½ cup fresh cold water

3 tablespoons sweet Mirin

4 tablespoons freshly squeezed limejuice

1 teaspoon fish sauce

1 teaspoon grated lime zest

1 teaspoon finely minced fresh green chili

3 tablespoons roughly cut cilantro

¼ teaspoon freshly ground black pepper

½ teaspoon paprika

DEVEIN the shrimp by removing the tails from the head. Remove the sand trail from the back of the shrimp by slicing through the center of the back lengthways ⅓ of the way through the shrimp. Rinse and pull apart each shrimp into several pieces with your fingers. Then trim any fat off the yellowtail, and slice into strips ½ inch wide and 1 inch long. Add to shrimp and chill.

IN a bowl combine all of the wet ingredients and whisk lightly to ensure that there are no lumps of coconut cream. Then add the lime zest, green chili, 2 tablespoons of the cilantro, and half of the black pepper. Whisk gently and set aside (This can be done up to 6 hours before serving). Add the seafood 1 hour before serving, giving the acid enough time to tenderise and cook the seafood. Chill until serving. To serve as small appetizers, place 2 heaping teaspoons of the shrimp and a drizzle of sauce into 12 shot glasses. To serve as a starter place 2 heaping tablespoons of the shrimp in a martini glass with a drizzle of the sauce. Sprinkle with the remaining cilantro and ground black pepper. Dust lightly with paprika and serve chilled.

Rack of New Zealand Lamb   Chef de Maison
with Port-Wine and Calvados Jus
with a Parsnip Mash and Grilled Asparagus

YIELD: 6 SERVINGS

A staple dish from Maule's homeland.

3 racks of New Zealand or Colorado lamb frenched and chimed (8 bones)

2 sprigs rosemary

12 sprigs thyme

2 tablespoons whole grain mustard

5 tablespoons extra virgin olive oil

5 cloves garlic minced

2 tablespoons whole coriander seeds, crushed

Salt and pepper

3 large onions with skin on

2 tablespoons tomato paste

1 cup of Calvados

2 cups of Port

2 cups red wine (Merlot or Cabernet Sauvignon)

4 bay leaves

2 quarts beef stock

1½ pounds parsnips

2 tablespoons salted butter

½ cup fresh pouring cream (sour cream will work as well)

⅛ teaspoon nutmeg

freshly ground black pepper

1 pound fresh trimmed asparagus

½ teaspoon lemon pepper

PREHEAT the oven to 375° F. Trim the lamb (keep the trimmings of the lamb, but not the fat, for the sauce). Combine the leaves of the rosemary and thyme with the mustard, 2 tablespoons olive oil, 3 cloves of minced garlic, the crushed coriander seeds, and a pinch of salt and pepper. Mix into a paste. Then spread the paste on the lamb, without covering the bones.

HEAT 3 tablespoons of the olive oil in a heavy skillet (cast iron is preferable) until it is shimmering; place the lamb racks meat-side down next to each other. Cook until golden (4–5 minutes). Then turn the meat over and place in the oven for approximately 15 minutes for medium rare, or 18 minutes for medium. Remove from oven and allow meat to rest for 6–7 minutes before slicing between the bones.

PAN-FRY the lamb trimmings in a solid-based pan until dark in color. Add 2 chopped onions with the skin on and cook out for 5 minutes. Add 2 cloves of minced garlic and cook for 2 more minutes. Add the tomato paste, cook for a further 2 minutes, and then add the Calvados (watch your eyebrows!) and then the port and the wine. Allow to reduce for 5 minutes before adding the bay leaves and beef stock. Simmer for 1½ hours and strain. Season to taste.

BOIL the parsnips in salted water until well cooked. Strain well; add 1 tablespoon butter, the pouring cream, nutmeg and a few grinds of cracked pepper. Purée in a food processor until smooth.

BLANCH the asparagus in boiling water for only 1 minute, then refresh immediately in an ice bath. Dry and season with 1 tablespoon melted butter, lemon pepper and salt. Grill the asparagus on a barbeque and serve hot. (The asparagus can be cooked beforehand and reheated in the oven.)

WITH all of the components hot, place the parsnip mash on the center of a hot plate. Arrange the 4 cutlets of lamb on the mash, lay the asparagus over the lamb and drizzle the sauce over the lamb. Garnish with a sprig of thyme.

SALAD OF ARUGULA, ENDIVE AND BABY SPINACH LEAVES WITH GOAT CHEESE, CARAMELIZED NASHI PEAR AND TOASTED CASHEWS, SWEET AND SOUR APPLE VINAIGRETTE

Chef de Maison

YIELD: 6 SERVINGS

Enjoy the delicious combination of flavors.

2 whole Belgian endives

4 cups arugula (alive and organic if possible)

4 cups fresh organic spinach

1 Nashi pear

2 teaspoons liquid honey

4 tablespoons Mirin

½ cup toasted cashews

3 tablespoons extra virgin olive oil

1 teaspoon Dijon mustard

1 tablespoon apple cider vinegar

2 sprigs of thyme

Salt and pepper

½ cup goat cheese

fresh cracked pepper

CUT the base of the endive and separate the leaves. Gently wash with the arugula and spinach, dry thoroughly and refrigerate. Clean and slice the pear in half, remove the seeds and slice into ½ inch slices. Place the pears into a smoking hot skillet. Cook both sides until colored and add the honey. Deglaze with 2 tablespoons Mirin and remove from the pan. (Keep the skillet to deglaze for the dressing.) Toast the cashews in a hot skillet until golden in color. Whisk the olive oil and mustard, add the Mirin, vinegar and leaves of the thyme. Deglaze the skillet with the dressing. Add salt and pepper to taste and set aside.

GENTLY toss the leaves in the vinaigrette and place on the centre of the plate, getting as much height in the salad as possible. Place the pears on next. Crumble the goat cheese over the salad and sprinkle with the cashew nuts. Crack fresh pepper over the salad and serve immediately.

Millefeuille of Mixed Berries, Cinnamon-Honey Mascarpone and Kirsch Sabayon

Chef de Maison

YIELD: 6 SERVINGS

Everyone will love this delightful dessert.

10½ ounce puff pastry	3½ ounces water
5 tablespoons powdered sugar	4 ounces kirsch
6 ounces Mascarpone cheese	2 pints raspberries
1 tablespoon honey	1 pint blueberries
⅛ teaspoon cinnamon	1 pint blackberries
3 egg yolks	6 sprigs of mint to garnish
3½ ounces granulated sugar	

ROLL puff pastry into ⅛ inch thickness and cut into 3½ inch squares or circles and refrigerate for 1 hour. Preheat oven to 400° F. Carefully place the pastry on a non-stick tray and dust with 1 tablespoon of powdered sugar using a fine sieve. Bake for 15–17 minutes until golden brown. Allow pastry to cool. Cut each piece of pastry in half horizontally through the center, creating a base and a lid for your dessert. Mix 6 ounces of Mascarpone with 1 tablespoon of liquid honey and ⅛ teaspoon of cinnamon. Chill mixture until serving.

MIX 1 pint of raspberries and 4 tablespoons of powdered sugar in a bowl, allow the berries to sit until the liquid draws from the berries. Purée the berries and pass through a fine sieve.

AT the time of assembly, lightly mix the egg yolks in a metal bowl with the granulated sugar, water and kirsch. Over a double boiler, whisk the mixture vigorously to a stiff peak, use caution not to overcook, as the eggs will scramble. Evenly distribute the Mascarpone onto the base of the pastry. Place in the center of the plate and cover each base with the remaining fresh berries. Drizzle the raspberry coulis over the berries. Whisk the sabayon to a stiff peak then immediately pour over the fruits, place the pastry lid on top and garnish with fresh mint leaves.

Tracey Van Curan

FOODS OF VAIL GOURMET

Tracey arrived in Vail, fresh out of business school in 1979. By 1980, she had started her fledgling catering business with only a handful of clients. An opportunity to study and apprentice with one of the largest catering companies in Southern California, under the direction of Elaine Beaubien, presented itself and off she went. Returning with a vast knowledge of artistic table designs and menu concepts, she set forth to expand her business. A summer spent in France, studying French Cuisine with Madeleine Kammen, helped to satiate her desire to learn as much as she could about the world of fine foods. Foods of Vail Gourmet is the wonderful culmination of many years of hard work and dedication to a career that she loves.

Foods of Vail Gourmet is a full service, Off Premise Catering and Event Planning business. It also boasts of a Gourmet Retail Shop where you can pick up Prepared Dinners, a nice selection of Frozen Appetizers, Imported and Artisan Cheeses, Homemade Soups, Olive Oils, Vinegars, and so much more.

Our commitment to our clients is to provide professional planning services, custom designed menus, trained chefs, and attentive wait staff. Our 23 years of catering successful events in the Vail Valley is a testimony to this philosophy.

Foods of Vail Gourmet is located at 150 E. Beaver Creek Boulevard in Avon, Colorado.

Tortellini with Lemon Artichoke Sauce

Can be served as a main course or a side dish.

½ cup fresh peas (frozen may be substituted)

½ cup julienned carrots

¼ cup virgin olive oil

1 cup sliced red onion

1 cup canned artichoke hearts

1½ cups heavy cream

1 teaspoon grated fresh lemon zest

1 tablespoon fresh lemon juice

2 to 4 tablespoons fresh dill (dried may be substituted)

salt and white pepper to taste

3 cups pre-cooked cheese tortellini

2 tablespoons freshly grated Parmesan cheese

2 tablespoon chopped fresh parsley

BLANCH the fresh peas in boiling water for approximately one minute, remove and run under cold water to retain their color. Add the julienned carrots to the boiling water and blanch until crisp-tender, approximately 1–2 minutes. Remove and run under cold water.

HEAT olive oil in large skillet over medium/high heat. Add the onion and cook until tender, add the artichoke hearts and turn up the heat. Cook the liquid out of the artichoke hearts and brown them slightly. Add the heavy cream and bring to a simmer, and cook till slightly thickened. Add the peas, carrots, lemon zest and juice, dill, and season with salt and pepper. Add the tortellini and cook until the tortellinis are heated through, about 3–5 minutes. Put in serving bowl and sprinkle with Parmesan cheese and parsley.

FOODS OF VAIL CHICKEN SALAD

YIELD: 6 TO 8 SERVINGS

One of the top sellers at Foods of Vail Gourmet Market!

4 cups of cooked chicken breast, cut
  into cubes

½ cup minced red onion

1 cup minced celery

1 cup chopped Gala or Fuji apple

¾ cup red grapes, cut in half

¾ cup toasted sliced almonds

1½ cups of mayonnaise (add more
  if it is too dry)

¼ cup Hibiscus or pear vinegar

salt and white pepper to taste

Mix all ingredients together and adjust the seasoning.

Chicken Satay with Thai Peanut Dipping Sauce

YIELD: 4 TO 6 SERVINGS

A great appetizer for any gathering.

3 boneless skinless chicken breasts

1 can coconut milk

1 tablespoon chopped fresh cilantro

salt and pepper

6 inch wooden skewers

Cut the chicken into strips and thread onto the wooden skewers. Be careful not to leave a big gap at the eating end of the skewer. Lay flat in a shallow dish. Cover with the coconut milk, cilantro, and salt & pepper. Marinate for 1 hour in the refrigerator. Either grill the chicken on barbeque grill or pan sear in a hot iron skillet till the chicken is slightly browned and cooked all the way through. Serve with the peanut sauce.

Thai Peanut Dipping Sauce

3 tablespoon Red Curry Paste

1 tablespoon minced garlic

2 tablespoons vegetable oil

1 cup water

2 tablespoons fish sauce

24 ounces sweetened coconut milk
   (Coco Lopez)

4 cups smooth peanut butter

½ cup soy sauce

½ cup limejuice

½ cup light brown sugar

Cook curry paste and garlic in the oil for 5–6 minutes. Add the remaining ingredients and simmer for 30 minutes or until reduced by 30%. Either drizzle over cooked chicken skewers or offer in a bowl as a dipping sauce.

CARROT-GINGER SOUP WITH CILANTRO CORIANDER CREAM

YIELD: 6 SERVINGS

A special soup to serve as a first course.

2 cups coarsely chopped onion	1 teaspoon coriander
1½ tablespoons minced fresh ginger	1 teaspoon paprika
2 garlic cloves minced	3 cups or more of chicken broth
dash of dried thyme and oregano	1 cup heavy cream
2 tablespoons vegetable oil	salt and white pepper
3 pounds carrots, peeled and chopped	

SAUTÉ the onion, ginger, garlic, thyme and oregano in the olive oil over medium low heat. Put a lid on the pot and sweat the onions until they are soft. Add the carrots, coriander, and paprika then pour in the chicken broth. Simmer until the carrots are very tender, about 30 minutes or so. Purée in blender and return to the pot, it will not be perfectly smooth. Add the heavy cream and season with salt and pepper. Serve warm topped with Cilantro Coriander Cream.

Cilantro Coriander Cream

1 cup sour cream
¼ cup chopped fresh cilantro
½ teaspoon coriander
½ teaspoon paprika
salt and pepper to taste

COMBINE all ingredients and serve a dollop over soup.

Christopher Wing

GAME CREEK CLUB AND RESTAURANT

Relatively new to Game Creek, but not new to creative fine dining, Colorado or even Vail Resorts, executive chef Christopher Wing has had a culinary career that spans not only years but many styles of food. From the development of a distinctive style in California's Bay Area to early Asian Fusion in Hawaii to discovering historical Colorado foods, Wing has devoted himself to presenting dishes that make sense in unique locations. Game Creek is just such a location.

Surrounded with spectacular views and drawing from the alpine ambiance and climate of the Vail Valley, Game Creek is the sort of setting that inspires a creative chef. "Working in this setting suggests wild game braised with juniper berries and black currant ale to me," says Wing. "Not heavy mountain foods laden with butter, but grilled salsify, sweet pea shoots, quince relish and lightly smoked trout. And, of course, just a taste of chocolate with apricots and cherries to compliment a port."

Before assuming his current position, Wing served as executive chef at the AAA four-diamond award-winning Keystone Ranch. He is credited with building the Ranch's reputation through his distinct culinary style that focused on using indigenous products and heirloom produce which created there a turn-of-the-century feel with fine porcelain, oriental rugs and knowledgeable service. He also served on the administrative and developmental side of food and beverage for many years as corporate executive chef for Keystone's nineteen fine dining, convention, casual and ski area restaurants.

A graduate of the University of California at Berkeley with a bachelor's degree in philosophy, Wing began his culinary career at the first of the avant-garde Berkeley restaurants in the "foody revolution" of the early '70s, turning from French to indigenous California products, style and techniques. He then took this orientation to Hawaii where he opened the award-winning restaurant, The Tamarind at the luxurious Waiohai Hotel on Kauai. There he combined local and Asian ingredients with French technique to

develop a fusion style before fusion was stylish.

In addition to working as a chef, Wing has also contributed to a number of cookbooks and participates in culinary fund-raising events for local and national charities, has taught culinary classes for Colorado Mountain College, spoken before the American Dietetic Association and is an American Culinary Federation Certified Executive Chef.

The Game Creek Club serves Contemporary American cuisine in an incredible setting. Located in the scenic Game Creek Bowl, Game Creek offers an unforgettable dining experience. Ride the Eagle Bahn Gondola to Eagle's Nest where you'll be taken by snow cat to the European-style mountain chalet. A multi-course meal featuring regional specialties, fresh seafood, fresh baked breads and homemade desserts await. Superb service and an outstanding wine list will enhance the evening's enjoyment. For reservations or information, please call 970-479-4275.

EGGPLANT TAPANADE

YIELD: 6 TO 8 SERVINGS

A minced salad of grilled eggplant used as relatively lean spread for bread. The Eggplant Tapanade uses an ingredient we use extensively at Game Creek and that is a garlic confit . . . simply whole garlic cloves simmered in olive oil to lightly cook it and thereby give it a mellow flavor.

1 cup olive oil	1 teaspoon anchovy paste
½ cup red wine vinegar	1 teaspoon mixed garlic confit
2 tablespoons basil pesto	½ teaspoon fennel seed
2 tablespoons minced capers	1 eggplant, thickly sliced with skin on
2 tablespoons whole grain Dijon mustard	freshly ground black pepper, Tabasco, salt

MAKE a vinaigrette with the oil, vinegar and seasonings. Pour over the eggplant to marinate. Grill the eggplant and then mince finely. Add pepper, Tabasco and salt to season. Serve with fresh bread.

PERUVIAN POTATO STRUDEL

Not a strudel in the Peruvian style, but a potato strudel made from purple potatoes from original Peruvian seed stock. The recipe makes a strudel log that is baked whole, then cut to reveal a startling purple center . . . great as an accompaniment to a steak or rack of lamb.

1½ pounds whole purple potatoes	1 cup sour cream
2 tablespoons minced fresh herbs	salt and freshly ground pepper
½ cup butter	1 prepared piecrust dough or dough sheet

SIMMER the potatoes in salted water for 30 minutes or until very tender. Drain and let dry while adding herbs, butter, sour cream, salt and pepper. Roughly chop or mash to incorporate seasonings…you should have many large pieces. When potatoes are cool, roll out pastry on floured board and add potatoes on top. Roll up strudel into a log and brush with water. Bake at 350° F for 20 minutes or until brown. Slice off 1½ inch pieces when ready to serve.

Tyrolean Country Tart

A farmhouse-style plum tart baked with Gorgonzola cheese. The crust is actually an almond batter that envelopes the plums and cheese . . . serve it with port wine . . . and leftovers don't last long.

4 ounces butter

4 ounces sugar

½ pound almond paste

1 egg

2½ ounces bread flour

2 eggs

6 ripe plums with stone removed, sliced

6 ounces crumbled Gorgonzola or
  other blue cheese

½ cup toasted sliced almonds

oiled or wax paper

9-inch removable bottom cake pan or
  spring form pan

COMBINE first four ingredients. Mix until it becomes a smooth paste. Add the remaining eggs and flour then mix again until well combined. You can store this mixture for days in a covered plastic tub. When ready to bake, place in cake pan lined with oiled paper or wax paper, lay plum slices and crumble Gorgonzola cheese over the top. Bake at 350° F for about 25 minutes or until it becomes golden brown. Let cool, run a knife around sides of pan to unmold, then press toasted almonds into sides of tart to finish.

Chocolate Hazelnut Torte with Cherries

A rich chocolate cake . . . dense and flavorful.

4 ounces unsalted butter

8 ounces semi-sweet chocolate chips

¼ cup hazelnut liqueur

2 egg yolks

1 tablespoon flour

2 egg whites, whipped

½ cup heavy whipping cream

¼ cup sugar

1 cup white chocolate chips

1 cup tart frozen cherries

½ cup toasted hazelnuts, cracked
   between plastic wrap with a mallet

Parchment paper

Springform pan

MELT butter and semi-sweet chocolate chips in saucepan over low heat. Add liqueur, yolks and flour. Fold in whipped egg whites. Line a 7-inch spring form pan with parchment paper on bottom and fill with mixture. Bake at 250° F for 30 minutes. Cool and refrigerate.

MAKE a white chocolate ganache by bringing heavy cream, sugar, white chocolate chips and cherries to a simmer. Fill the indentation in the cake with the white chocolate ganache.

WHEN cool, run a sharp warm knife around the inside of the spring form pan and open to remove the torte. Decorate sides of cake with cracked toasted hazelnuts. Cut thin slices with hot knife.

Iranian and Trout Caviars with Crème
Fraîche and Chervil-Potato Blinis
(*Larkspur Restaurant, page 52*)

Oven Roasted Liberty Duck
with Root Vegetable Stuffing
and Cranberry Relish
(*Larkspur Restaurant, page 48*)

(L)

Colorado Organic Tomato Tower with
House-Made Mozzarella and Basil
(*Larkspur Restaurant, page* 45)

American Apple Pie with Vanilla Bean
Ice Cream and Concord Grape Sauce
(*Larkspur Restaurant, page 50*)

Stephen Virion

LA BOTTEGA

tephen Virion began his career in the hospitality business at the age of 15 working as a prep cook in a busy business lunch restaurant in Wilmington, Delaware. In 1976 he attended the Culinary Institute of America in Hyde Park, New York, where he received the groundwork for a career in the culinary arts. During the years building up to the opening of La Bottega, he has worked and traveled throughout the United States and Europe.

Stephen initially worked at the Hotel duPont in Delaware. His desire to work abroad was quickly rewarded when he accepted a position *La Bottega* at the Carlton Elite Hotel in Zurich. He moved to Vienna, Austria, to work at the Hilton Vienna where he worked in the 2-star Michelin restaurant Prinz Eugen. It was in Vienna where he met and married his wife and partner of La Bottega, Elisabetta. Elisabetta was born in Asiago, Italy. Stephen went on to work other various restaurants in Europe including Chef at Villa Arceno in Tuscany, Consulting Chef at Harrods in London, Jacques Maximin in Nice, Restaurant Troisgros in Roanne and Jean Bardet in Tours.

In the United States, Stephen worked at the Four Seasons in Philadelphia, The Pump Room in Chicago and the Swissotel in Chicago.

Stephen and Elisabetta moved to Vail in November 1994 after having accepted a position at the Vail Village Inn working for Josef Staufer. In November 1997 they opened up La Bottega in a small corner space on Meadow Drive. They specialized in a variety of quick and affordable meals, which encompassed a diverse clientele. In January of 1999 they expanded into the adjacent space. The menu expanded to include stone oven pizzas, homemade pastas and a variety of fish and meat dishes based on Italian cuisine.

In August of 2001 they again expanded to add Vail's first wine bar with emphasis on Italian wines, but also including a large variety of wines from other great wine producing regions.

Stephen and Elisabetta reside in Vail with their children, Stephanie and Valentina.

La Ribollita (White Tuscan Bean and Vegetable Soup)

La Bottega

YIELD: 6 SERVINGS

This scrumptious soup is a favorite in Vail.

For the beans:
1 pound dry cannellini beans

1 medium onion, cut into quarters

1 celery stalk

1 medium carrot, peeled and cut
  into pieces

several garlic cloves

1 sprig rosemary

2 sage leaves

salt

For the soup:
3½ ounces extra virgin olive oil

2 Spanish onions, sliced

1 or 2 dried chilies, chopped fine

2 ripe tomatoes, peeled, seeded and
  coarsely chopped

1 tablespoon tomato paste

1 leek, cut into small dice

3 celery stalks, cut into small dice

2 medium carrots, cut into small cubes

2 cloves crushed garlic

2 stalks rosemary

4 sage leaves

2 bunches red Swiss chard

salt and freshly ground white pepper

6 slices stale bread for serving

Soak the beans overnight in cold water. The next day drain well and place in a heavy casserole with the ingredients designated for the beans. Bring to a slow boil. Remove the foam as it rises to the top of the liquid. When the majority of the foam has been removed, add salt. Let simmer for approximately 4 hours until the beans are tender. Remove the majority of the beans leaving some whole. Place into a food mill and purée. Reserve in a bowl with the beans that are remaining.

Place the oil into a heavy bottom casserole and add the onions and chilies then let cook slowly until tender. Add the remaining vegetables and sauté until tender. Add the tomatoes and the tomato paste and cook for several minutes. Place the bean purée into the mixture (it should be fairly runny, if not, add more water.) Add the sage and rosemary and let mixture simmer for approximately 2 hours. Stir the pot often to keep the bean mixture from sticking to the bottom. Season to taste. This soup is best if let to stand overnight. When ready to serve, place a small slice of stale bread that has been rubbed with garlic in the bottom of each soup bowl. The soup can then be ladled over the bread heated or as typically done in Tuscany, served at room temperature. Thinly sliced onions can be served with the soup along with a very fresh extra virgin olive oil drizzled over the top of the soup.

ROASTED ALASKAN HALIBUT WITH PAN SEARED FOIE GRAS OVER STEWED MORELS WITH WILD ASPARAGUS

La Bottega

YIELD: 6 SERVINGS

Full of flavors and a wonderful meal.

1 pound fresh morel mushrooms

olive oil to sauté

1 ounce minced shallots

4 ounces Sauvignon Blanc

1 cup double strength chicken stock

4 tablespoons chilled sweet butter, cut into cubes

½ ounce tarragon leaves

2 pounds wild asparagus (substitute thin asparagus)

1 cup ice water

1 cup rice flour or all-purpose flour

canola oil for frying

6 (6 ounce) portions of Alaskan Halibut (skin removed)

6 (2 ounce) slices fresh duck foie gras

salt and freshly ground white pepper

RINSE the morel mushrooms in cold water to remove any sand. If necessary, split lengthwise to ensure that all sand and debris has been removed. In a medium sauté pan, add olive oil (do not overheat) and sauté the shallots until tender. Add the morels and cook until softened. Add the Sauvignon Blanc and reduce until all of the liquid has evaporated. Add the chicken stock and reduce to about ⅓ the original volume. Remove from heat and slowly stir in two tablespoons of butter a small amount at a time. Chop ½ of the tarragon and add to this mixture.

TRIM the bottoms of the asparagus and place the asparagus into a pot of boiling salted water until al dente or still crunchy to the bite. Immediately place into a bowl of ice water to stop the cooking process. Keep 24 of the asparagus spears on the side. Take the chilled water and add flour until it is the consistency of a batter. Season the batter with salt and keep very chilled.

PRIOR to preparing the fish, take the 24 spears of asparagus and season them with salt and pepper. Place canola oil into a saucepot and heat to 350° F. There should be enough oil to tempura fry the asparagus. Once heated, dredge the asparagus into the chilled batter and fry until golden brown. Remove and place on a screen to drain.

SEASON the halibut filets with salt and pepper. Add 3 teaspoons olive oil to a sauté pan and place the fish in the pan once hot. Let brown and then turn onto the other side. Place into a 400° F oven for 6 to 8 minutes depending on the thickness of the fish.

HEAT a thick-bottomed pan (preferably an iron pan) to sauté the foie gras. Season the duck foie gras and place into the hot skillet. Brown quickly on both sides keeping the foie gras medium rare. Remove and place the foie gras on a cookie rack.

TAKE the remaining asparagus and sauté in 2 tablespoons of butter until heated through.

IN six large pasta or soup bowls, place the stewed morel mushroom mixture with the liquid divided between the bowls. Take the sautéed asparagus and place on top of this mixture. Place the roasted halibut on top and then the foie gras on top of the fish. Drizzle some of the rendered fat from the foie gras over the top. Finish with tempura-fried asparagus and garnish with remaining tarragon leaves.

CRISPY VEAL SHANK WITH ROASTED VEGETABLES ON CANNELLINI BEANS

La Bottega

YIELD: 6 SERVINGS

The braised veal turns out extra juicy.

For the beans:
1 pound dry cannellini beans
1 medium onion, quartered
1 celery stalk, chopped
1 medium carrot, chopped

1 sprig sage
1 sprig rosemary
3 garlic cloves
salt

For the Veal Shanks:
6 veal foreshanks (approximately
   18 ounces)
3 carrots cut in batonette-like for crudite
3 stalks celery cut in batonette
2 red onions, peeled and cut into wedges

8 garlic cloves
6 sprigs rosemary
salt
freshly ground black pepper

SOAK the beans in cold water overnight. Next day drain the bean and place in a heavy pot. Cover with water until approximately twice the volume of water to the beans. Bring to a boil stirring occasionally so the beans do not stick to the bottom of the pot. Skim the foam off that forms on the surface and discard. When most of the foam has risen to the top add 2 teaspoons of salt and the vegetables under the recipe for the beans. Let cook gently until the beans are soft. Remove from heat and strain.

WHILE the beans are cooking, place some olive oil in a heavy bottomed braiser and heat. Season the shanks with salt and pepper. Place the shanks in the braiser and brown well on all sides. Remove from pan. Add the vegetables and roast until tender and roasted brown without burning. Season lightly. Place the shanks on top of the vegetables and place a rosemary sprig on top of each shank. Cover braising pan with aluminum foil and place in 325° F oven. Braise for 2½ to 3 hours until the shanks are tender.

WHEN ready to serve, heat oven to 475° F and place the uncovered shanks and vegetables in oven for about 10 minutes or until the outside of the shanks become crisped. If necessary, add a small amount of water if the natural juices appear to be drying up.

TOSS the beans lightly in extra virgin olive oil and season with salt and pepper then warm. Portion the beans onto the middle of six good-sized plates. Place the shanks on top of the beans and the roasted vegetables over the top of the shanks. Spoon the natural juices over the top of the vegetables and garnish with a sprig of rosemary. Serve with a nice Italian Pinot Noir. Buono Appetito!

SUMMER TIRAMISU

YIELD: 6 SERVINGS

Always the perfect ending to a great Italian meal.

6 tablespoons rum	**2 egg whites**
6 tablespoons milk	**24 ladyfingers**
3 egg yolks	**6 ounces meringue**
3 tablespoons sugar	**chocolate shavings and cocoa powder**
10 ounces mascarpone cheese	**to garnish**

MIX the rum and milk together. Beat the egg yolks with the sugar until very pale and soft. Fold in the mascarpone cheese a little at a time until a smooth consistency. Whisk the egg whites until stiff and fold into the mascarpone and egg yolk mixture.

LINE the bottom of a serving dish with half of the ladyfingers. Taking a pastry brush, soak the ladyfingers with half of the milk and rum mixture. Take one third of the mascarpone mixture and spread over the ladyfingers. Break the meringue into pieces and spread onto the layer of mascarpone. Cover with another third of the mascarpone mixture and repeat the ladyfingers on top of this layer and soak with remaining milk and rum mixture. Top with remaining mascarpone.

CHILL for several hours or overnight. When ready to serve, top with chocolate shavings and sprinkle on the powdered cocoa.

Paul D. Ferzacca

LA TOUR RESTAURANT

His career has been extensive from Spiaggia Restaurant, The Ritz Carlton Hotel-Chicago, Hotel Intercontinental, The Racquet Club of Chicago, Two Elk Restaurant in Vail, and Game Creek Club in Vail. In 1991, Ferzacca arrived in Vail as Executive Chef of The Two Elk Restaurant atop Vail Mountain's China Bowl at the elevation of 11,250 feet. The challenge of cooking in high elevation did not stop Ferzacca. He transformed on-mountain resort dining in the ski industry. Offering exquisite food to some 4,000 to 6,000 hungry skiers each day, Ferzacca immediately gained rave reviews from the culinary press with articles in *Bon Appetit, SKI, Snow Country, New York Times, Nations Restaurant News, Chef, Rocky Mountain News, Denver Post* and all local newspapers.

1995 brought a new challenge for Ferzacca, with the opening of the exclusive Game Creek Club on Vail Mountain. The fine dining chalet seats some 175 members for elegant lunches and in the evening for a multi-course fixed menu.

His love and passion for his career became evident nationally with his invitation to cook at the James Beard House in New York City. While fulfilling his duties with Vail Resorts Inc. he was also an adjunct chef instructor at the Vail-based Johnson and Wales University — the only ski resort culinary school in the world.

In 1998, Ferzacca fulfilled his life long dream and became Chef/Owner of the famous La Tour Restaurant. Ferzacca has turned this landmark in Vail Village into the most elegant, contemporary French restaurant in the Vail Valley.

Ferzacca is a native of Chicago, Illinois, studied both Architecture and later Restaurant Management in college and holds a degree from the Culinary School of Kendall College. He has received awards of excellence on his wine list by the Wine Spectator. He was the feature chef of the 1997 — Taste of Vail. In October 1999 he was honored in Norfolk Virginia as the feature chef for The Chesapeake Bay Wine Festival. One month later in November 1999 he was the feature chef for Mexico's Puerto Vallarta, Gastronomic Festival. In November of 2000 Chef Ferzacca was one

LA TOUR

CONTEMPORARY FRENCH CUISINE

of the feature chefs for the Vail Valley Wine Auction. Always trying to further educate himself and bring knowledge to his staff, Chef Ferzacca in September 2000 passed his certificate level with the Court of Master Sommeliers.

Ferzacca moved to Vail for the love of the recreational lifestyle, which he enjoys with his wife, Lourdes and two children JonPaul 10 years and Nina 5 years.

La Tour Restaurant is a French American restaurant located in the Vail Village. La Tour features French American cuisine in a warm friendly atmosphere. La Tour is surely a "diamond in the rough" amongst an array of restaurant choices available, simply a "must" when dining in Vail.

Chef Ferzacca and his wife Lourdes have decorated the interior with bright, rich colors, fresh flowers and have local and nationally recognized artwork adorning the walls. But, the most important point is Ferzacca's mouth watering French American cuisine and an award-winning wine list. The cuisine is light, contemporary French utilizing the highest quality products available. The

menu changes with the season and always features new exciting dishes. As Chef Ferzacca would say *"Simplicity is the mother of beauty."* That's exactly the type of food you will find at La Tour, simple elegant food that tastes great. The wine list featuring French and American wines has been honored with the "Award of Excellence" by the *Wine Spectator,* with close to 300 selections of some of the best wines available, you are bound to find one you like.

Chef Ferzacca and his family invite you to enjoy the finest French Cuisine in the Vail Valley. La Tour was voted best French Restaurant in the Vail Valley according to the Vail Daily Readers Poll. Chef Ferzacca has been honored at the James Beard House in New York as one of the best-undiscovered chefs in the Country. His standard of quality and consistency is unsurpassed.

Reservations are preferred: 476-4403. La Tour is available for private, corporate parties and buy-outs. Children are always welcome. The outdoor patio offers excellent dining a la fresco. La Tour is a non-smoking environment.

Escargot in Sauce Persillé (French Helix Snails cooked in Parsley Sauce)

YIELD: 4 SERVINGS

After dining all over France, this is simply the best preparation of snails that Chef Ferzacca has ever had.

24 Large French Helix Snails (usually available canned)

6 ounces whole unsalted butter

4 shallots, minced

8 cloves of garlic, minced

1 cup dry Vermouth

2 cups heavy cream

2 bunches parsley, washed and finely chopped

salt to taste

white pepper to taste

Open snails, drain and rinse well. In large sauté pan over medium heat; using 2 ounces of whole butter, sauté snails, shallots and garlic until shallots are opaque in color, do not caramelize shallots or garlic. Once shallots are opaque add the vermouth and let reduce by half. Once wine is reduced by half add the heavy cream and parsley and let reduce to sauce consistency or "nap." (Sauce should coat the back of a spoon.) When the sauce is nap turn off the stove and mount the remaining butter into the sauce and finish with salt and white pepper to taste.

FIELD GREEN SALAD WITH TOASTED GOAT CHEESE, DRIED CRANBERRY, PINE NUTS, WHOLE GRAIN MUSTARD VINAIGRETTE

LA TOUR

CONTEMPORARY
FRENCH CUISINE

YIELD: 4 SERVINGS

This salad will soon become one of your mainstay salads in your repertoire.

4 ounces goat cheese	1 cup all purpose flour
1 whole egg	1 cup breadcrumbs
1 tablespoon milk	2 ounces pure olive oil

SLICE the cheese into 4 one-ounce pieces. Place in freezer until very hard. Prepare breading station; mix egg and milk in a bowl to create an egg wash. Place flour in a separate bowl and place the breadcrumbs in a separate bowl. Once cheese is hard, dredge in flour then egg wash then breadcrumbs. Place back in freezer. You can prepare the cheese up to three days in advance. To toast the cheese remove from freezer and sauté over high heat with pure olive oil just enough to toast the bread crumbs, about 30 seconds each side. Remove from pan and place on paper towel. You can now refrigerate the cheese until ready to serve salad.

Whole Grain Mustard Vinaigrette:

1 shallot	1 tablespoon Champagne vinegar
1 clove garlic	½ teaspoon kosher salt
1 teaspoon whole grain mustard	¼ teaspoon ground white pepper
1 teaspoon honey	3 tablespoons extra virgin olive oil

MINCE the shallots and garlic and combine with the mustard, honey, vinegar, salt and white pepper in small stainless steel bowl. Slowly add the extra virgin olive oil in a small stream while whisking to completely emulsify the vinaigrette. Once all oil is incorporated, taste the vinaigrette to check the seasoning add more salt or pepper if needed.

4 teaspoons pine nuts

1 teaspoon each, fresh fine herbs —
  chervil, parsley, tarragon, chives

4 ounces mixed greens

1 head Belgium endive (8 large leaves)

8 pearjolais tomatoes (or any substitute)

4 teaspoons dried cranberries

kosher salt to taste

ground white pepper to taste

Toast the pine nuts in a 350°F oven for about 4 minutes or until golden brown. Once toasted let cool completely. Prepare fines herbs: rough chop all herbs (chervil, parsley, chives and tarragon), mix together and reserve to season salad. Make sure greens are clean, if not wash in cold water in a large bowl. Dry the greens very well. Cut about 1 inch off the bottom of the Belgium endive and peel off 8 leaves to garnish the salad. Cut the pearjolais tomatoes in half and reserve to garnish salad. Once you are ready to serve salad to your guest, heat up goat cheese in oven at 350°F for about 5 minutes.

In a large bowl, combine mixed greens, Belgium endive, fines herbs, kosher salt, ground white pepper and about 2 to 3 tablespoons of vinaigrette. Toss gently to combine and plate endive first on plate at 10 and 2 o-clock, place salad in middle of plate, place tomatoes at 5 and 7 o-clock and place warm goat cheese leaning up against salad at 6 o-clock.

Dover Sole Meunière with Haricots Vert, Baby Creamer Potatoes, Lemon Brown Butter Sauce

YIELD: 4 SERVINGS

"La Tour's signature dish, one that I could eat every night," says Chef Ferzacca.

- 8 baby creamer potatoes (you can substitute red bliss)
- 2 teaspoons salt
- 2 Roma tomatoes
- 4 ounces Haricots Vert, (you can substitute Green Beans)
- 4 ounces heavy cream
- 4 ounces unsalted whole butter
- 3 teaspoons chives
- 4 (1 pound each) whole Dover sole fish
- Kosher salt to taste
- ground white pepper to taste
- 1 cup all purpose flour
- 4 ounces clarified butter or canola oil
- 2 fresh lemons

PLACE potatoes in a small pot and cover with cold water. Add 2 teaspoons of salt and bring to a boil, once boiling turn down to a simmer and let cook until potatoes are fork tender. Remove from water and let cool on a sheet pan. Once cool refrigerate until needed. This procedure can be done one day in advance.

IN another 2 quart pot fill with water and bring to a boil. While that is coming to a boil, with small paring knife, remove the stems from the roma tomatoes and score an X on the other end of tomato to prepare them for blanching to remove the skin and seeds. Also, remove the ends of the haricots vert, and reserve for blanching. Set up an ice bath with plenty of ice and cold water to refresh the tomatoes and haricots vert once blanched. Once the water is at a rolling boil, blanch the roma tomatoes for about 15 seconds to just blister the skin and refresh in the ice bath. Remove from ice bath, let drain, keep ice bath to refresh haricots vert.

NOW season the boiling water with enough salt to make it taste like the ocean. This will retain the color of the beans when cooking. Note: green vegetables release acid into the water and the evaporation, which will discolor the vegetables. To counteract the acid an alkaline must be added to the water, salt is an excellent alkaline. Also do not cover the pot or the acid released in the evaporation will be dispersed back into the water. Once the water is back at a rolling boil and seasoned with salt, blanch the haricots vert for about 5 minutes or until al dente. The starches should be jelled completely when cooking any bean, to aid in the digestion process. Remove beans and refresh in ice bath. Once chilled again remove from water, let drain and reserve for plating. This step can be done one day in advance.

MAKE the brown butter sauce by combining the heavy cream and butter in a 2-quart saucepan, bring to a boil and reduce to simmer. Note: When bringing to boil stir occasionally and watch carefully so as the cream does not boil over. Once reduced to a simmer stir occasionally, allow to cook until the cream and butter breaks. Once the cream and butter breaks you must stir constantly to toast the milk solids until golden brown, this will happen quickly, be careful not to burn the milk solids. Once milk solids are golden brown remove from pan and allow cooling in a different container. Once cooled, but still liquid, purée in blender to break up milk solids. You can make the brown butter one week in advance and just reheat in a warm water bath when needed.

NEXT you can prepare the tomatoes by removing skin then cut into quarters lengthwise, remove seeds then dice the tomato fillets into ¼ inch pieces. Reserve in small dish for garnishing plate. To prepare the chives, slice into ⅛ inch pieces, reserve in small dish for garnishing plate.

REMOVE the skin from both sides of the fish and fillet the meat to yield 4 fillets from each fish. This can be done one day in advance. To plate the Dover sole, place brown butter sauce in a hot water bath and bring back up in temperature. Have a small pot of water on stove to reheat potatoes and haricots vert. Before cooking fish place potatoes and haricots vert in water and reheat. Once hot remove and season with salt and ground white pepper. Season fish with salt and ground white pepper, dredge in flour and sauté in clarified butter or canola oil until golden brown. Remove and place on plate with potatoes, haricots vert. Sauce the fish, potatoes and haricots vert with brown butter, garnish plate with diced tomatoes, chives and squeeze fresh lemon juice over everything.

CRÈME BRÛLÉE FLAMBÉ WITH
GRAND MARNIER MACERATED BERRIES

LA TOUR

CONTEMPORARY
FRENCH CUISINE

YIELD: 4 SERVINGS

*Wow your guests with a classic dessert that is easily flambéed. This recipe requires a
sifter and a propane torch.*

1 vanilla bean, whole fresh	¼ pint raspberries
16 ounces heavy cream	¼ pint blackberries
3 ounces sugar	¼ pint blueberries
3 egg yolks	2 ounces Grand Marnier
1 whole egg	½ cup granulated sugar
8 strawberries	1 ounce 151 Bacardi rum

PREHEAT oven to 325° F. Split vanilla bean in half and scrape out all beans inside, place
beans and skin inside a 2-quart pot. Add the cream and sugar. Scald the cream by bringing
the liquid to a boil. Be careful, as the cream will boil over. Keep a careful eye on the pot
and stir occasionally. While the cream is coming to a boil; crack your eggs into a stainless
steel bowl and whisk eggs until combined. Once cream is scalded temper the cream
into the eggs by very slowly adding the cream to the eggs and constantly stirring. Strain
the crème brûlèe batter through a fine chinois and ladle about 6 ounces into each of
4 crème brûlèe dishes. Place dish on a flat sheet pan, place in preheated oven. Add water
until it reaches half way up crème brûlèe dish. Bake crème brûlèe for about 45 minutes
or until the custard is firm. Remove from oven and let cool completely. Place in
refrigerator until needed for plating. The crème brûlèe can be made up to three days in
advance and kept in refrigerator. Slice strawberries into quarters and place in small
stainless steel bowl. Combine the blackberries, blueberries and raspberries to the
strawberries, add the Grand Marnier and let macerate about 30 minutes in refrigeruor.

WHEN ready to plate, remove crème brûlèe from refrigerator and sift sugar on top of
custard until a small amount creates a white coating. Brûlèe with propane torch until
the entire top is golden brown. Garnish the top of the crème brûlèe with the macerated
berries. Place a half of a capful of 151 Bacardi Rum on top of crème brûlèe and ignite
with a lighter. Make sure your guests let the alcohol burn off, do not blow out or eat
while on fire.

Thomas Salamunovich

LARKSPUR RESTAURANT

Dinner at Larkspur is a widely varied sensory treat of generous proportions. From the elegant surroundings at the base of Vail Mountain to the impeccable service and the wonderfully delicious fare, your dining experience will undoubtedly be one that you remember fondly for a long time to come.

Thomas Salamunovich and his wife, Nancy Sweeney, welcome you to their mountain creation with open arms. A warm, small-town atmosphere and friendly service await you when you join us for dinner, albeit with all of the style and quality of the finest metropolitan restaurants.

Larkspur's lush interior combines high style with just the right level of intimacy. The wine list is excellent and Chef Thomas Salamunovich's always-innovative contemporary American menu, never fails to surprise or delight.

Thomas Salamunovich, Owner / Executive Chef

As with so many great chefs, Thomas Salamunovich's culinary knowledge and skills have been learned and honed on the front lines of outstanding kitchens.

Following his humble beginnings as a line cook in Vail in 1981, Thomas graduated from the California Culinary Academy in 1984, and then attended the Culinary Institute of America at Greystone and the School for American Chefs. After graduation, he worked in San Francisco for Jeremiah Tower at Stars Restaurant and as Executive Sous Chef of Wolfgang Puck's Postrio.

Thomas also paid his dues in Europe, working in Paris and Lyon at renowned restaurants such as Paul Bocuse, Lucas Carton, and Elysee Lenotre, as well as a stint at the world-famous Poilane Boulangerie. He returned to Vail in 1993 as Executive Chef at Sweet Basil, and also designed, opened and operated Zino Ristorante in Edwards.

He has taught at the Cooking School of Aspen, been published numerous times, and given cooking demonstrations on CBS.

In late 1999, Thomas and his lovely wife Nancy opened Larkspur Restaurant, Bar & Market in the Golden Peak building at the base of the Vail Mountain resort, where his creative talent, flair and perfectionism continue to shine in this beautiful new showcase.

Larkspur has received the award of excellence from Distinguished Restaurants of North America (DiRõNA) as well as *Wine Spectator's* award of excellence for "having one of the most outstanding wine lists in the world."

www.larkspurvail.com

COLORADO ORGANIC TOMATO TOWER WITH HOUSE-MADE MOZZARELLA AND BASIL

(L)

larkspur

YIELD: 4 SERVINGS

One of Larkspur's most popular starters, the Tomato Mozzarella tower is available seasonally.

3 small balls of fresh mozzarella
extra virgin olive oil
freshly ground black pepper
3 Colorado organic tomatoes
6 ounces red wine vinaigrette
sea salt and coarse pepper

9 leaves fresh basil
2 handfuls rocket
4 slices toasted ciabatta bread
1 ounce basil pesto
1 tablespoon balsamic syrup (reduced by
   three-quarters)

SLICE mozzarella balls into 4 slices. Sprinkle each slice with extra virgin olive oil and freshly ground black pepper. Slice tomatoes into 4 slices. Lay tomatoes on a sheet-pan and sprinkle with vinaigrette, sea salt and coarse pepper. Lay one piece of mozzarella on each tomato slice. Place one leaf of basil on each piece of cheese. Place one of the tomato, cheese, and basil pieces on top of another. Repeat again to create 3 layers. Reserve. On a plate, place a small handful of rocket in the center. Pour a little of the red wine vinaigrette onto the rocket. It will spill out onto the plate. Place a piece of the ciabatta bread onto the rocket and drizzle a little pesto onto the bread. Drizzle a little of the balsamic syrup around the bread. It will pool into the vinaigrette. Transfer one of the tomato towers onto the bread. Sprinkle a little black pepper around the plate and drizzle extra virgin olive oil over the entire dish. Repeat the procedure for the remaining 3 plates.

Red Wine Vinaigrette

2 ounces red wine vinegar
¼ clove garlic chopped
Pinch of sugar

Salt and pepper to taste
4 ounces olive oil blend

COMBINE all ingredients, except the oil, in a bowl. Whisk in salt and pepper to taste. Drizzle the oil into the bowl while whisking.

Butternut Squash Soup with Pumpkin Seed Oil, Fried Sage and Beet Powder

(L)

larkspur

Something to warm the soul on a wintery day.

Butternut Soup:
1 large butternut squash	1 teaspoon chopped ginger
2 ounces butter	1 quart quality chicken stock
salt and pepper	4 ounces cream
1 white onion diced	1 teaspoon honey
1 large carrot, peeled and diced	pinch nutmeg

Beet Powder:
½ cup finely chopped beet

Garnishes:
1 tablespoon pumpkin seed oil	8 leaves of fried sage (canola oil for frying)
1 tablespoon toasted pumpkin seeds	1 teaspoon finely chopped chives

For the soup, cut the butternut squash in half and brush with ½ ounce of butter. Sprinkle with salt and pepper and bake face down on a sheet pan in a 400° F oven until completely soft. Cool and remove the meat from the skin. Reserve. Sauté the onion and carrot in the remaining butter until soft and free of color. Add the chopped ginger, squash meat and chicken stock. Bring to a boil, and reduce to a simmer. Simmer for 30 minutes and blend with a hand blender. Add cream and strain. Adjust seasoning and add honey and nutmeg. Cool soup and refrigerate one day to develop flavors before warming and serving.

For the beet powder, dry the beet purée in a towel and place on parchment paper in the microwave on low setting until completely dried. Roughly 30 minutes. Put in a spice grinder and grind to fine powder.

FOR the sage leaves, heat canola oil in a sauté pan and fry leaves until crispy but not colored. Remove from oil, sprinkle with a little salt and set on a paper towel to drain.

TO serve, heat soup until just boiling and ladle into a large soup bowl. Drizzle the pumpkin oil, chives, beet powder, and pumpkin seeds over the top of the soup. Arrange 2 sage leaves in the center. Repeat with remaining 3 soups.

Oven Roasted Liberty Duck with Root Vegetable Stuffing and Cranberry Relish

(L)

larkspur

YIELD: 4 SERVINGS

Larkspur's unique twist on Thanksgiving dinner.

Liberty Duck:

4 liberty duck breasts	salt and pepper to season

Stuffing:

1 carrot, peeled and diced	3 cups diced artisan whole wheat bread
1 celery root, peeled and diced	2 tablespoons chopped parsley
1 turnip peeled and diced	1 teaspoon chopped thyme
1 white onion, peeled and diced	3 ounces chicken stock
2 stalks celery, diced	3 ounces butter

Relish:

½ pound fresh cranberries	½ cup sugar
1 orange peeled and seeded	2 ounces orange juice
1 teaspoon ginger	pinch of salt

Sweet Potato Purée:

2 large sweet potatoes	1 ounce cream
1 granny smith apple, peeled and diced	pinch nutmeg
2 ounces butter	salt and pepper to taste

Sauce:

16 ounces Marsala	1 teaspoon black peppercorns
1 quart brown chicken stock	1 ounce apple cider vinegar
3 roughly chopped shallots	1 ounce canola oil

FOR the stuffing, toast the bread on a sheet pan in the oven until lightly browned. Set aside. Put all of the vegetables in a large pot with the butter and stew for 30 minutes until all the vegetables are soft. Add the herbs, bread, and stock and lightly stir. Season to taste and hold warm.

FOR the relish, put all of the ingredients in a food processor and blend until well incorporated. Set aside.

FOR the sweet potato purée, roast the sweet potatoes until soft. Remove the flesh and blend with the cream, nutmeg and salt and purée and adjust seasoning. Hold warm.

FOR the sauce, sauté the shallots and peppercorns in the canola oil until lightly colored. Add the Marsala and reduce by ¾. Add the chicken stock and reduce by half. Strain, add vinegar, adjust seasoning and hold warm.

TO serve, season the duck on both sides. Sauté in a dry pan on the fat side down until crispy and well rendered. Flip over duck and sear until the breast is medium rare. Hold warm for 5 minutes to let rest and then slice in thin strips across the grain. Put the stuffing in the middle of the plate, fan duck around front part of stuffing and place a spoonful of each the relish and sweet potato purée around the backside of the stuffing. Spoon sauce around the plate. Repeat with remaining 3 plates.

AMERICAN APPLE PIE WITH VANILLA BEAN ICE CREAM AND CONCORD GRAPE SAUCE

(L)

larkspur

YIELD: 6 SERVINGS

Larkspur reinvents an American tradition created by Larkspur Pastry Chef Allana Smith.

Apple Filling:

8 granny smith apples, peeled and finely diced

2 cups apple cider

¼ cup flour

1 cup light brown sugar

1 teaspoon ground cinnamon

½ teaspoon ground nutmeg

¼ teaspoon ground allspice

¼ teaspoon cloves

½ vanilla bean

COMBINE all ingredients in a heavy bottom saucepot and set over medium heat. Stirring occasionally cook until apples are soft (approximately ½ hour.) Cool.

Pie Dough: yields 12 circles, 2½ inch in diameter

2⅓ cups pastry flour

1 cup plus 1 tablespoon cold butter, cubed

1 teaspoon salt

3 tablespoons plus 1 teaspoon cold water

1 egg

1 tablespoon cider vinegar

COMBINE salt and flour, cut in cubed butter until pea-size. Add liquids to dry ingredients and butter, until mixture comes together. Roll out dough on a lightly floured surface until approximately ⅛ inch thick. Cut dough into circles with a 2½ inch diameter round cutter. Let dough chill on a non-stick baking sheet and then bake at 350° F for 8–10 minutes until golden brown. Cool. Set aside.

Crumb Topping:

3 cups oats

1 cup brown sugar

1 cup butter, cold, cubed

¾ cup flour

2 teaspoons cinnamon

MIX all ingredients together until butter is pea-size.

Concord Grape Sauce:

3 cups Concord grape juice

PUT in a small saucepot on medium low heat, let reduce until only ½ cup remains. Cool.

Vanilla Bean Ice Cream:

PURCHASE your favorite vanilla bean ice cream and pre-scoop 3 cups of ice cream into oval balls. Set aside in freezer.

Assembly Directions

6 rings 2½ inch diameter   **6 sugar sticks**
1 baking sheet   **6 spice cookies**

PLACE rings on baking sheet. Put one baked circle of pie dough in each ring. Top with enough apple filling to reach almost the top of the ring. Top with crumb topping. Heat in a 350° F oven for 5 minutes. Place individual rings on each plate and lift rings from pies. Pool sauce around the pie and top with vanilla ice cream, a sugar stick, and a spice cookie.

Iranian and Trout Caviars with Crème Fraîche and Chervil-Potato Blinis

(L)

larkspur

YIELD: 4 SERVINGS

You don't need to reserve champagne and caviar just for special occasions.

Blinis:

12 ounces Yukon gold potatoes

3 tablespoons all purpose flour

4 tablespoons crème fraîche

2 eggs beaten

2 whipped egg whites

salt and pepper to taste

20 small chervil sprigs

Caviars:

1 ounce Iranian osetra caviar

1 ounce trout caviar

Crème fraîche:

1 teaspoon buttermilk

1 cup heavy cream

FOR the blinis, bake the potatoes until cooked through. Rice while warm and mix with sifted flour. Work until incorporated and mix in the whole eggs and salt and pepper. Do not overwork. Add the whipped egg whites. Cook small spoonfuls on a buttered griddle as you would pancakes. Place a small piece of chervil on top of each blini before flipping over.

FOR the crème fraîche, bring both ingredients to room temperature. Incorporate and let sit at room temperature for one day. Cover and place in refrigerator for one day. Stir before placing in serving bowl.

TO serve, pour the Iranian caviar onto a mother of pearl plate and then mound the trout caviar in the middle of that. Place the mother of pearl plate on top of crushed ice placed in a bowl. Use a mother of pearl spoon to serve the caviar. Serve the blinis on a warm plate and place the crème fraîche in a container beside them.

Colorado Rack of Lamb
with a Calypso Beans,
Vegetable Crust Basket
and Cranberry Lamb Jus
(*Mirabelle at Beaver Creek*)

Crème Brulée Flambé with
Grand Marnier Macerated Berries
(*La Tour Restaurant, page* 42)

Dover Sole Meunière
(*Mirabelle at Beaver Creek, page 55*)

Clockwise from top left: Field Green Salad with Toasted Goat Cheese, Dried Cranberry, Pine Nuts, Whole Grain Mustard Vinaigrette (*La Tour Restaurant*, *page* 38); Wine Room (Larkspur Restaurant); **Mangos, Coconut Bavaroise with Raspberry Coulis** (*Mirabelle at Beaver Creek*)

Daniel Joly

MIRABELLE AT BEAVER CREEK

Belgian born Master Chef Daniel Joly graduated from the Culinary Institute of Brussels in 1986. He trained at the best tables of renowned Belgian restaurants, such at Comme Chez Soi and Barbizon.

After a short stop in South Carolina, Daniel arrived in Beaver Creek as chefmanager for Mirabelle Restaurant in 1992. He and his wife Nathalie purchased Mirabelle in April 1999, Mirabelle and chef Joly's unique cooking style have been acclaimed by numerous publications and institutions such as Wine Spectator, the James Beard House, Zagat, Mobile (four stars), Ski Magazine and Bon Appetit, to mention just a few. Chef Joly also hosts the popular "Something's Cooking with Daniel" on Vail's TV8.

Chef Joly is a certified Belgian Master Chef and takes great pride in his work but if you ask him what gives him the most satisfaction of all his awards and accomplishments he will simply say that awards and peer recognition are great, but a customer complimenting him for a great dining experience is the best of all. "That is what keeps me going, I enjoy making guests happy . . . That is why I love cooking and what I do".

Mirabelle Restaurant is located at the entrance of Beaver Creek. The charming ranch house has been a wonderful place for many events ranging from large corporate events, weddings, rehearsal dinners to smaller private birthday parties and family reunions. Cocktail and butler passed hors d'oeuvres are served in the spring, summer and early fall on our front lawn and porch. In the winter months our guests enjoy our bar area and fireplace for cocktails.

We can host smaller groups as well as those as large as 150 to 200 people. The main dining room can seat up 60 to 70 guests, the adjacent French room can seat 30 to 40 guests. The East room can seat up to 28 guests. Groups have requested a tent, dance floor or other seating arrangements. Our staff will be more than happy to assistant you in any way to make your event unforgettable.

www.mirabelle1.com

VEGETABLE RAVIOLI WITH ASPARAGUS COULIS

"A wonderful vegetarian dish with lots of colors". . . from Chef Daniel Joly.

1 bunch asparagus

2 cups heavy cream

1 teaspoon freshly ground nutmeg

salt and pepper to taste

1 carrot, peeled and finely chopped

1 red pepper, finely chopped

1 stalk celery, finely chopped

1 shallot, minced

2 tablespoons olive oil

1 tablespoon fresh cilantro, chopped

1 package won ton sheets

1 egg, lightly beaten

BLANCH asparagus, combine with cream, nutmeg, salt and pepper in blender then strain mixture and reserve. Sauté all vegetables with olive oil, herbs, salt and pepper until tender. Lay won ton shells out on a cutting board. Place 1 tablespoon vegetable mixture in the center of each sheet. Brush the edges with egg wash and fold over in a diagonal. Repeat procedure until you use all of the vegetable mixture. Blanch in hot, salted water for 3 minutes. Serve in bowl with asparagus coulis.

DOVER SOLE MEUNIÈRE

YIELD: 4 SERVINGS

Dover Sole is native to the North Sea and it has a very unique flavor.

4 (12 ounce) Dover Sole

4 Yukon gold potatoes

5 cups baby spinach

½ cup flour

½ stick butter

salt and pepper

juice from 2 lemons

¼ cup fresh chopped chives

CLEAN sole by removing skin from top and bottom of fish. Make a cut at the base of the tail and scrape back skin towards head. Grab skin and pull towards head. Flip fish over and repeat process. Remove head and skin. Remove top and bottom fins by cutting from head to tail. Remove the insides of the fish and clean in cold water. Set aside.

CLEAN, peel and quarter the potatoes lengthwise. Tourner each quarter. Cook potatoes in boiling water until almost tender. Set aside.

BRING a small pot of water to a boil. Clean baby spinach and place in boiling water for 3 minutes. Remove from boiling water and place in ice-cold water. Set aside.

LIGHTLY flour and season sole. Melt butter in sauté pan and place sole in pan for 4 minutes per side. Add lemon juice and chives. Meanwhile, sauté potatoes in buttered pan. Lightly sauté spinach. When fish is cooked, carefully remove filets from the bone — there are two on top and two on the bottom. Place a small amount of sauce from the pan on each serving plate. Arrange filets in the middle of the plate with spinach on one side and 4 potatoes on the other side. Garnish with chives and serve immediately.

GRILLED LOBSTER FRICASSEE WITH GARLIC SAUCE

YIELD: 4 SERVINGS

"This is a wonderful dish that incorporates many different flavors . . ." is Joly's lasting impression.

3 Yukon gold potatoes

4 pounds live Maine lobster (steamed)

1 cup virgin olive oil

salt and pepper

1 shallot, finely chopped

½ pound chanterelle mushrooms

2 cloves garlic, roasted

2 cups vegetable stock

3 tablespoons unsalted butter

PEEL and dice potatoes. Cook in lightly salted boiling water for 5 minutes. Potatoes will pierce easily when done. Remove from water. Set aside. Remove lobster meat from tail and claws. Coat with olive oil, salt and pepper. Place the meat on the grill. Grill each side for a few minutes rotating half way through to create crisscross grill marks. Set aside. In a non-stick sauté pan, sauté the finely chopped shallot, mushrooms and roasted garlic. Sauté for a few minutes and gradually add vegetable stock. Bring to a boil. Add three tablespoons of butter and bring back to a boil. Once the butter has incorporated, it will make a smooth sauce. Add the potatoes and the lobster. Serve in a large bowl with salt and pepper.

Warm Crêpes with Golden Apples

YIELD: 4 SERVINGS

"A great childhood memory and a typical 4:00 p.m. snack in Belgium . . . Just delicious" says Chef Daniel Joly.

2 golden apples
1 cup flour
4 eggs
1 cup sugar

2 cups milk
2 tablespoons butter
brown sugar
whipping cream

PEEL and core the apples, but leave the apples whole. Slice the apples into ⅛ inch thick pieces crosswise so that you get apple wheels or wafers. Set aside.

IN a bowl whisk together flour and egg, adding one egg at a time. When the mixture is smooth, add the sugar and milk slowly to avoid lumps forming. Let stand for 20 minutes.

WARM a 12-inch pan with butter over medium heat. Add three apple wafers and brown on one side. Flip the apples and pour batter over them. Cook each crêpe for about 2 minutes and flip to the other side briefly. Stack the crêpes on a plate with brown sugar in between or garnish with your preference of whipped cream, ice cream or fresh fruit.

Piney River Ranch

We take mountain dining to a whole new level with our unique holiday outing to Piney River Ranch! A magnificent holiday feast, which includes prime rib and roast turkey with all the trimmings, will amaze you. We have a sledding hill, snowshoe trails and the most stunning skating rink in North America. Perfect activities to work up that Holiday feeling and appetite. All gear is provided at no extra charge. In addition, your transportation to the Ranch will be in the world's most versatile vehicle, the HUMMER, outfitted with specially designed snow treads by Mattracks! It is a 10-mile ride to the lake through breathtaking mountain scenery.

The Piney River Ranch has so much to offer everyone for every season! Bikers sojourn the road to Piney Lake, fishermen come to fish the river or the lake, hikers come to experience every kind of walk or climb, horse lovers come for their favorite Alpine ride, photographers flock to this picturesque land, painters compose masterpieces, families come to relax for the day, canoers paddle on reflected waters, wedding couples come to take their vows in paradise, bird watchers watch, hunters come for the game, snowmobilers take the ride of their lives, snowshoers find peace in the glistening white snow. There is to be room for everyone, and everyone is smiling!

We would like to continue to provide an opportunity for people to come and enjoy Piney River Ranch, but in ways never available before. We have brought in cabins and teepees so people can stay overnight and witness the gorgeous sunrises, sunsets, and moonlit nights. We invite families and corporations to plan retreats at Piney River Ranch and we are expanding the services provided for weddings and other family events.

Make your special day unforgettable in our Rocky Mountain paradise. Make your sacred vows in the most picturesque setting this side of heaven. Our unique lakeside wedding deck reaches out onto the pristine waters of Piney Lake with the

PINEY RIVER RANCH ™

Gore Range as a backdrop. Plan something small for a simple site fee, or use a wedding planner for an elaborate event, we will expertly handle all the arrangements you may need.

At Piney River Ranch we will gladly accommodate any special requests for private or group functions. Our covered lakeside pavilions, lodge, and restaurant can accommodate groups of all sizes; only the clear mountain sky is the limit. And our executive chef will prepare a delicious menu, with outstanding expertise in Western cuisine.

Treat your guests to all of the Ranch activities at your next family gathering or corporate retreat. Kids will have the time of their lives staying in our overnight Tepee Village while you enjoy the serenity of our lakeshore cabins. We offer several family/group packages with meals and activities included.

PINEY RIVER RANCH CHEESY ARTICHOKE DIP

P|**R**
|**R**
PINEY
RIVER
RANCH™

YIELD: 8 TO 10 SERVINGS

A nice warm appetizer — any crowd will empty the bowl.

1 (12 ounce) can of artichoke hearts	1 cup finely diced red onion
2 cups grated Parmesan cheese	¼ teaspoon paprika
½ cup mayonnaise	⅛ teaspoon cayenne pepper
½ cup sour cream	¼ teaspoon ground cumin
¼ cup chopped chives	⅛ teaspoon curry powder
¼ cup chopped parsley	¼ teaspoon of both salt and pepper

PREHEAT the oven to 350° F. Roughly chop the artichoke hearts. Add all of the remaining ingredients together and mix well. Then add mixture to the artichokes and place into a 9x6 Pyrex oven dish. Bake for 35–40 minutes uncovered, until golden brown. Serve in a bowl with bagel chips or Melba toast for dipping.

GRILLED PORTOBELLO MUSHROOM SANDWICH WITH GOAT CHEESE AND TANGY MAYONNAISE

YIELD: 6 SERVINGS

Another wonderful example of a tasty lunch.

6 Portobello mushrooms

2 tablespoons olive oil

pinch of salt and pepper

3 ounces sweet soy sauce

3 ounces balsamic vinegar

2 ounce Mirin

3 sprigs of fresh thyme

1 tablespoon mayonnaise

1 tablespoon sour cream

juice from ½ lemon squeezed

1 tablespoon Dijon mustard

⅛ teaspoon paprika

⅛ teaspoon cayenne pepper

1 cup roasted red or yellow peppers

6 ounces goat cheese

12 slices olive bread (fresh from the bakery)

2 cups fresh arugula

PREHEAT the oven to 350° F. Peel the mushroom and trim off the stalk. Place the mushroom stalk-side down into a hot pan with the olive oil, and add a pinch of salt and pepper. Cook for 2 minutes then add the soy sauce, balsamic, Mirin and thyme. Cover with aluminum foil and place the entire pan into the oven. Bake for 15 minutes and set aside to cool and absorb the remaining juices.

FOR the tangy sauce, mix the mayonnaise, sour cream, lemon juice, mustard, paprika and cayenne in a bowl and season with a pinch of salt and pepper to taste. Place the roasted peppers and goat cheese on top of the mushroom and heat in the oven for 5 minutes. Toast the bread and spread the tangy sauce on each slice. Place the mushroom on the bottom slice of bread and lay arugula on top. Drizzle the remaining juices from the pan over the leaves, place the top slice of bread on the sandwich and slice it in half. Serve with a favorite salad.

Kevin Nelson

TERRA BISTRO

Kevin Nelson's culinary career started on Long Island, where he grew up, and where he worked at several high volume small-town and beach-resort restaurants. Nelson moved to Vail in 1991, and was hired on at Terra Bistro in 1993. At Terra Bistro, under the creative guidance of Chef's Cynthia Walt and Tim Graybill, Nelson discovered a passion for a healthier approach to quality cuisine. He found their innovative insights to be the perfect nourishment for his own creative appetite, and he quickly adopted their unique and health-minded flare. Throughout his career Nelson has continued expanding his knowledge researching techniques and cuisines of different cultures to adapt in his menu creations. Chef Kevin trained at Long Island University and Farmingdale University, and he has attended continuing education courses at the Culinary Institute of America. Nelson has assisted Chef's preparing for events at the James Beard House in Manhattan, and he has been featured in several local publications.

Terra Bistro is one of Vail's finest restaurants offering a delicious mix of seasonal produce, organic meats and poultry, and fresh seafood. Terra Bistro continues to be an award-winning restaurant with accolades including the DiRoNA Award, the Wine Spectator's Award of Excellence and wonderful attributes from many national critics. Terra Bistro recently expanded the restaurant space to include a lower level with excellent views of Gore Creek. This new space is perfect for private parties and wedding receptions. Terra Bistro is located in the Vail Mountain Lodge & Spa. Please call 970-476-6836 for reservations.

Ice Cold Gazpacho with Dungeness Crab Salad and Crème Fraîche

YIELD: 2 SERVINGS

You will impress your friends with this recipe.

1 cup peeled ripe tomatoes, rough chop	1 teaspoon olive oil
¼ cup sundried tomatoes, re-hydrated	¼ teaspoon sherry vinegar
¼ cup roasted red peppers, peeled, seeded and rough chopped	⅛ teaspoon Tabasco sauce
	1 small ripe tomato, small dice
1 cucumber, peeled and seeded, ½ rough chopped and ½ small dice	1 tablespoon red pepper, small dice
	¼ ripe avocado, small dice
½ cup light vegetable stock	3 tablespoon Dungeness crab meat
2 tablespoons red onions, rough chop	1 tablespoon crème fraîche*
1 tablespoon red onions, small dice	ground cumin and ground coriander to taste

Sour cream can be substituted for crème fraîche.

KEEP all diced vegetables separate from the rest of the ingredients. Purée everything else in a blender or food processor except crab, crème fraîche, avocado, and spices. Season the purée with salt and let stand in the refrigerator for at least 1 hour.

MIX the crème fraîche with the cumin and coriander.

WHEN the tomato purée is well chilled, mix in all of the remaining diced vegetables except the avocado. Serve the gazpacho in two cold soup bowls. Garnish with the crab, the crème fraîche, and the avocado.

California Sea Bass Braised with Lemon and Basil in Tomato Consommé, Served with a Smoked Salmon Risotto Cake and Garnished with Parsley Relish

YIELD: 2 SERVINGS

Not only delicious, but a beautiful presentation as well.

For the Risotto Cakes (to be prepared ahead of time):

3 cups water or vegetable stock	1 cup Arborio rice
2 ounces white wine	1 teaspoon minced parsley
2 tablespoons olive oil	½ teaspoon fresh minced thyme
½ teaspoon fresh minced garlic	salt and pepper to taste
1 tablespoon fine diced red onion	2 tablespoons smoked salmon, diced
1 tablespoon finely diced carrot	¼ cup breadcrumbs

FIRST heat the vegetable stock and white wine together to a simmer and keep hot throughout remaining steps. In a separate shallow saucepan, heat the olive oil over medium to high heat and add the garlic, onion, and carrot and sauté until the onions are translucent. Add the rice and sauté for approximately 2 minutes. Add approximately 2 ounces of the hot broth to the rice and stir continuously until all liquid is absorbed into the rice. Reduce heat if needed. Repeat until all broth is used and absorbed. Remove from heat and add fresh herbs and season to taste. Let the risotto cool and then add the minced salmon. Shape the cold rice into two cakes and dredge in the breadcrumbs.

For the Tomato Consommé (to be prepared ahead of time):

1 quart roma tomatoes, rough chopped	1 ounce fresh basil
1 quart water	

ROAST the tomatoes in a roasting pan at 375° F for one hour. Transfer to the stovetop and add the water and basil. Let steep for 45 minutes on very low heat. Strain through a fine mesh sieve or cheesecloth.

For the Parsley Relish (to be prepared ahead of time):

¼ cup fresh parley, rough chopped

4 capers

½ teaspoon diced red onion

2 teaspoons extra virgin olive oil

¼ teaspoon fresh lemon juice

salt and pepper to taste

COMBINE all ingredients in a food processor and reserve chilled.

For the Braised Fish:

2 (6 ounce) pieces of fresh sea bass

2 tablespoons olive oil

2 tablespoons diced zucchini

2 tablespoons diced yellow squash

2 tablespoons diced roma tomatoes

1 tablespoon diced sundried tomatoes

2 cups tomato consommé

1 tablespoon lemon zest

½ teaspoon fresh lemon juice

2 tablespoons chopped scallions

1 tablespoon basil chiffonade (very thin slices)

salt and pepper to taste

For the garnish:

2 fresh lemon segments (rind and pith removed)

PREHEAT the oven to 400°F. In a medium sauté pan over high heat, sear the fish in olive oil for approximately two minutes on both sides. Add the zucchini, squash, tomatoes and sundried tomatoes. Then add 2 cups of the tomato consommé, the lemon zest, and lemon juice. Transfer the whole pan to the oven and let cook for 8 to 10 minutes. Sear the risotto cakes in olive oil until golden on both sides. Reduce the heat and let the cakes cook for 6 to 8 minutes, turning occasionally.

To serve, place the risotto cakes in large noodle bowl or entrée bowl. Remove the fish from the oven and with a spatula place the fish on top of the rice cakes. To the sauté pan add the scallions and basil chiffonade and season to taste. Spoon the vegetables and broth around the fish. Garnish with a small dollop of parsley relish and one lemon segment.

Venison Loin with Caramelized Onion Ratatouille, Sundried Tomato Demi-Glace, and Gorgonzola Gratinée

Mouthwatering to the very last bite!

Venison loin

1 shallot, minced

¼ teaspoon fresh thyme, chopped fine

¼ teaspoon fresh parsley, chopped fine

¼ teaspoon fresh rosemary, chopped fine

½ teaspoon sel gris (coarse wet sea salt)

¼ teaspoon fresh cracked pepper

1 teaspoon mushroom oil

½ teaspoon cooking Madeira

MIX all ingredients thoroughly and coat venison loin for marinade.

For the demi-glace:

1 cup beef demi-glace*

½ cup vegetable stock

¼ cup Madeira

1 large shallot, peeled and sliced

¼ cup sundried tomato halves

salt and pepper to taste

Demi-glace is a reduction that starts from beef stock and is slowly cooked until most of the water has evaporated and it is reduced to less than half its original volume thereby intensifying the flavor. If you would like to avoid the labor-intensive process, you could substitute 2 cups of canned beef broth and omit the vegetable stock.

COMBINE all ingredients in a saucepot and simmer on a medium flame until reduced by 25% let chill before blending. When cool, purée in a blender until well blended. It is important to chill the sauce before blending because too much heat could cause pressure to build up in the blender and create a big mess. If your sauce seems too thick, slowly add vegetable stock while blending until desired consistency.

For the ratatouille:

1 cup red onion, peeled and chopped

½ cup white pearl onions, peeled and quartered

¼ cup sundried tomatoes, re-hydrated and chopped

1 tablespoon olive oil

2 tablespoons Marsala wine

2 tablespoons fresh spinach, roughly chopped

SAUTÉ onions and tomatoes in the oil until onions are translucent and begin to caramelize. Move pan away from heat and deglaze with Marsala then return to heat and add spinach. Cook until all liquid evaporates.

GRILL venison loin to preferred done-ness and re-heat the sundried tomato demi-glace. Sprinkle one side of a dinner plate with 1 teaspoon quality bleu cheese or Gorgonzola crumbles then set plates in the oven for a few minutes to allow the cheese to melt somewhat. Next spoon onion ratatouille in center of plate then ladle the sauce on the side of the plate without the cheese. Slice the venison loin and fan out over sauce and ratatouille.

White Bean and Squash Sauté

YIELD: 2 SERVINGS

A vegetarian delight and a Terra Bistro mainstay.

3 tablespoons olive oil

3 tablespoons finely diced carrots

3 tablespoons finely diced celery root

¼ cup finely diced leeks

2 sweet winter squash (delicata or butternut) peeled, seeded, cubed and roasted

3 tablespoons finely diced sundried tomatoes

3 tablespoons dry white wine

1 cup vegetable stock

1½ cups great northern beans, cooked until soft

4 cippolini onions peeled, blanched and roasted

4 pickled artichoke hearts cut in half and roasted

1 Japanese eggplant, sliced in half lengthwise and grilled

2 teaspoons butter

1½ tablespoons combination of chopped fresh sage and thyme

1 tablespoon quality crumbled Gorgonzola cheese

Heat oil in a large sauté pan and add carrots, celery root and leeks, cook for 2 minutes then add squash, sundried tomatoes, white wine and vegetable stock. Let vegetables and broth simmer for a 2 minutes and add the beans. Heat the cippolini onions, artichoke hearts and eggplant for a few minutes in the oven. Let the beans cook and the liquid reduce for a few minutes and add the butter and herbs. Serve the bean dish in large entrée bowls and arrange the artichokes and onions around the top of the beans with the eggplant half in the middle. Garnish with the crumbled Gorgonzola.

INTERNATIONAL

Flavors

TCHOUCHOUKKA

YIELD: 4 TO 6 SERVINGS

This dish is best served cold and makes a fantastic starter or can be served as a side dish with cold meat. Tchouchoukka is from North Africa and it is based on tomatoes, peppers and garlic. The recipe comes from Claudine Tordjeman and her father, Marcel Tordjeman's family from Miliana, Algeria.

1½ bulb of garlic
1½ tablespoons olive oil
8 pounds of canned, peeled tomatoes,
   or fresh tomatoes if in season

10 red peppers,
salt and pepper

FIRST peel the garlic and slice it as thin as possible, then you pour the oil in a saucepan and let the garlic color slightly (not brown). Once the garlic is slightly colored, add the tomatoes and let them reduce. In the meantime, you need to grill the peppers either on the barbecue or under the grill in the oven. Turn the peppers regularly until the skin turns completely black. Once they are black on all sides, remove from the grill and arrange them on a plate, wrap them in newspaper or put the peppers into a plastic bag until they cool down to a point where you can handle them without burning yourself. By wrapping the peppers in newspapers or placing them in a plastic bag, it will be easier to peel the peppers. Once the peppers are cool, peel them using your fingers only and remove the seeds. It is important to not wash the peppers. Once they are peeled and deseeded, cut the peppers in pieces of about ¾ of an inch and add them to the tomatoes which are still cooking. Reduce the fire under the tomatoes, garlic and peppers to the minimum and let it cook for up to 2 to 3 hours on a very, very low temperature on the stove, as if you were cooking a jam. Add the salt and pepper to taste. The end result should be a sort of a jam consistency of tomatoes, peppers, and garlic. Make sure it doesn't stick to the bottom of the saucepan. Actually the longer you cook it the better the flavor becomes. The original amount of tomatoes and peppers will reduce by half if not more.

SHRIMP SALSA DIP

YIELD: 8 TO 12 SERVINGS

A simple, and delicious dip that comes from Janell Connors in North Bend, Oregon. The Shrimp Salsa is great with tortilla chips — especially the blue corn tortilla type.

½ to 1 pound fresh shrimp meat	1 can diced green chiles
2 tomatoes diced and drained	1 teaspoon oregano
1 to 2 cups catsup (to taste)	dash of garlic salt
2 avocados chopped	2 tablespoons lemon pepper
2 bunches green onions chopped	1 to 4 tablespoons picante sauce

RINSE and drain shrimp meat. Drain the chopped tomatoes in a colander to keep the mixture from becoming too soupy. Mix all remaining ingredients together. Refrigerate until cool. Serve as a dip with tortilla chips.

BLUE CHEESE VICHYSSOISE

YIELD: 5 SERVINGS

Adding blue cheese to this traditional recipe gives a whole new dimension and a wonderfully zesty flavor. This recipe comes from Whitney Williams Jones of Pepper Pike, Ohio.

3 tablespoons butter	2 cups chicken broth
2 medium onions, thinly sliced	1 cup light cream
1 teaspoon minced garlic	⅓ cup heavy cream
3 medium potatoes, peeled and cut into 1-inch cubes	½ cup crumbled blue cheese
	salt and pepper

IN a large saucepan melt the butter, add the onions and cook until the onions are soft but not browned. Add the potatoes, stir and cook for 5 minutes. Add the chicken stock and bring to a boil. Reduce the heat to low, cover and simmer until the potatoes are tender, about 30 minutes. Let cool. Add both creams and gently reheat the soup, but do not boil. Stir in ½ cup of blue cheese. Blend the soup in batches until smooth. Season with salt and pepper. Serve hot or cold and garnish with extra blue cheese.

Spicy Garbanzo Bean and Chicken Sausage Soup

YIELD: 6 SERVINGS

This easy recipe makes a very hearty après ski meal from local Amy Chesterton.

1 teaspoon olive oil

1 package pre-cooked chicken sausages (4), casings removed and crumbled (Gerhardts brand works great — you can use any flavor)

4 garlic cloves, minced

1 (28 ounce) can crushed tomatoes (you can also use tomatoes with added spices)

1 (4 ounce) can diced green chiles

1 teaspoon ground cumin

1 teaspoon dried rosemary, crumbled

3 (16 ounce) cans garbanzo beans, drained and rinsed

1 to 2 cups vegetable broth

HEAT olive oil in Dutch oven, or other large pot, over medium-high heat. Add crumbled sausage (can be broken up with a fork in pan) and garlic. Cook approximately 5 minutes, until sausage is slightly browned and cooked through. Add crushed tomatoes, green chiles, cumin, and rosemary. Simmer 10 minutes, stirring occasionally. Add garbanzo beans and vegetable broth — bring to a boil. Reduce heat and simmer for 15 minutes. Season to taste with salt and pepper.

Gulyás Soup (Gulyásleves)

YIELD: 6 TO 8 SERVINGS

Pronounced gooyaash, the word Gulyás means herdsman and this soup used to be the staple dish of Hungarian shepherds. There are many variations of this recipe but the basic dish is a soup with beef, onion, potatoes and paprika. Maria Taylor of London sends us this recipe from her Father's family recipe file.

1 large or 2 medium onions, chopped

1 teaspoon crushed garlic

2 tablespoons of vegetable oil

2 pounds cubed stewing steak

2 cups of red wine (or enough to cover the meat in the pan)

4 pints beef/chicken stock

2 carrots, thickly sliced

2 parsnips, thickly sliced

2 potatoes, quartered

1 large green pepper, chopped

3 or 4 bay leaves

1½ cups of flat leaf parsley

Gulyás cream (if you can find it anywhere)

1 tablespoon of mild paprika (plus an extra 2 teaspoons if you cannot find Gulyás cream)

2 teaspoons tomato paste

1 chili (medium heat), chopped

1 large teaspoon of caraway seeds (grind them in a pestle and mortar)

salt and pepper to taste

flour for dumplings

2 eggs

sour cream or crème fraîche to serve

Fry the onions in the oil until lightly browned then add the garlic and beef. Stir until the beef is lightly browned then add enough red wine to cover the meat. Cook over a low/medium heat until the wine has almost disappeared, spooning off any residue from surface if necessary, then add the stock, caraway seeds and bay leaves. Cover and cook for at least 30 minutes. Meanwhile, make the dumplings by putting enough flour into a dish with the 2 eggs, salt and pepper to taste. Knead until firm and leave to rest until the soup is made. Add carrots, parsnips, potatoes and the flat leaf parsley to the beef and let the soup simmer. After the first 10 minutes add the paprika, tomato paste, chili, green pepper, salt and pepper. When the soup is ready, tear really tiny pieces of the dough with your fingers and throw them into the soup. Bring the liquid to a rolling boil and when the dumplings are ready they will float to the top. Add a large dollop of cream to the pan and stir or, if you prefer, swirl a teaspoon of cream round the soup in the bowl before serving.

Smoked Salmon Pasta Salad

YIELD: 4 SERVINGS

From Deanne Siddall of Marblehead, Massachusetts comes this tasty salad. Deanne recommends using the traditional style of smoked salmon (comes in a chunk instead of slices) . . .

2 cups farfelle (bow tie pasta)

1½ cup sliced asparagus

1 (4 ounce) package smoked salmon

1¼ cup cherry tomatoes

⅓ cup feta

½ cup olive oil vinaigrette

¼ teaspoon salt

¼ teaspoon freshly ground pepper

BOIL pasta and add asparagus for the last few minutes. Drain and rinse the pasta and asparagus. Cut salmon into ½-inch strips. Combine remaining ingredients and toss gently. Enjoy!

SUMMER CUCUMBER SALAD

YIELD: 6 TO 8 SERVINGS

A great side salad perfect for any occasion comes from Rachel Sweet in Salt Lake City, Utah.

1 pound cucumbers

6 to 7 sprigs of fresh dill

2 green onions (scallions)

4 tablespoons olive oil

2 tablespoons grated Parmesan cheese

2 to 3 teaspoons balsamic vinegar

salt to taste

PEEL and slice cucumbers, thinly slice green onions, and finely chop dill — mix together in a medium sized serving bowl. Add oil, vinegar, cheese and salt. Cover and refrigerate until cold (2 or more hours is best).

CORNBREAD SALAD

YIELD: 8 TO 10 SERVINGS

A southern delight from Ellen and George Pace of London though the recipe is a part of the Beavers family collection in West Plains, Missouri.

1 package Martha White yellow cornbread mix	**1 small onion, diced**
1 package Martha White Mexican cornbread mix	**1 large tomato, chopped**
	1 cup Miracle Whip

FOLLOW directions for each cornbread mix and combine the two mixes. Bake according to the directions on the packaging. Crumble baked cornbread into a large mixing bowl. Add the diced onion and chopped tomato. Toss together with the Miracle Whip. Chill at least 3 hours before serving.

Janssons Frestelse (Jansson's Temptation)

YIELD: 4 TO 6 SERVINGS

This is a Swedish dish eaten in the wintertime, particularly at the holiday season. It's great served with Swedish meatballs, lots of beer and ice cold akvavit (schnapps) to cleanse the palate from the salty taste. This recipe comes from Christina Price Convis . . . there's hardly anything more typically Swedish than Janssons Frestelse, Jansson's Temptation. Today there's also a particular day set aside for honoring this dish. It's the last Friday in September.

2 onions, sliced

3 tablespoons butter

4 medium raw potatoes, peeled and cut into small strips

20 Swedish anchovy fillets (marinated sprats in a can)

1¼ cups cream

SAUTÉ onion in 1 tablespoon of butter. Butter the bottom and sides of 7½ x 11 baking dish. Layer potatoes, onion, and anchovy fillets, finishing with layer of potatoes. Pour over 1 tablespoon of brine from anchovy can and dot with remaining butter. Add half of the cream. Bake at 400° F for 50–60 minutes. Add remaining cream after 10 minuntes of baking time. Serve hot from baking dish. Smakliga maltid (Bon appetit)!

FRIED GREEN TOMATOES

YIELD: 6 SERVINGS

Not just a movie, but also a fun side dish for a barbeque or southern fried chicken . . . sent by Gloria Highers of Murfreesboro, Tennessee.

3 pounds green tomatoes (can substitute zucchini squash)	**2 cups cornmeal**
	salt and pepper to taste
½ cup vegetable oil	**ranch dressing to serve**

PICK tomatoes before they start to turn red. Remove the stem and slice the tomatoes. Pour vegetable oil into a skillet and heat (pretty hot). Mix cornmeal with salt and pepper then place on a plate or flat dish. Take sliced tomatoes and coat with cornmeal on both sides (make sure tomato slices are moist, so cornmeal will stick to them). Drop coated slices into hot oil and cook until golden brown on each side. Dip in ranch dressing (or dressing of your choice) or enjoy them plain. Zucchini squash may also be cooked like this.

COLD POACHED SALMON

YIELD: 8 SERVINGS

This rendition comes from the Complete Idiot's Guide to 20-Minute Meals *by Tod Dimmick (Alpha Books, 2003) Tod is a published author who resides in Dover, Massachusetts. On one memorable vacation in the highlands of Scotland, the Dimmicks were served cold poached salmon. It was elegant and delicious, and remarkably quick to make.*

1 (3-pound) salmon filet

Broth:

1 bottle of white wine (a dry white, such as a Sauvignon Blanc or Chardonnay)	**2 onions, chopped**
	3 bay leaves
water sufficient to cover the salmon after addition of the wine, about 10 cups	**2 teaspoons dill**
	2 teaspoons celery seed
1 tablespoon salt	**½ teaspoon ground black pepper**

THOROUGHLY rinse the fish. Using a fish poacher or large pan with lid, combine the broth ingredients, bring to a boil, and simmer for 5 minutes. Lower the fish into the broth (if you are not using a rack to hold the fish in the broth, cheesecloth is a good idea, wrapped around the filet, to keep it from breaking apart when you lift it out). Add more water if needed to cover the fish. Put on the lid and simmer 10–15 minutes, or until done.

REMOVE the fish carefully from the broth, and cool in the refrigerator. It is best to cool the salmon on a platter, and then slide it onto the serving tray atop a bed of greens (like kale) and garnish with lemon wedges and fresh dill.

BOBOTIE

YIELD: 6 SERVINGS

This is "A staple South African classic of Cape Malay origin brought to the country by the Malay slaves many years ago!" This delicious recipe comes from Andrew Walker of Bronxville, New York.

2 tablespoons vegetable oil

2 onions, peeled and roughly chopped

2¼ pounds good quality lean
   ground beef

1 very thick slice of white bread

1 cup milk

1 tablespoon curry powder (heat to taste)

1½ tablespoons sugar

2 teaspoons salt (or to taste)

½ teaspoon freshly ground pepper

¾ teaspoon tumeric

1½ tablespoons malt vinegar

½ cup seedless raisins or combination of
   raisins, dried apricot, and almonds

2 tablespoons strong chutney

2 bay leaves (or fresh lemon leaves
   if available)

2 medium eggs

PREHEAT oven to 350° F. Heat oil in medium sauté pan. Stir in onions. Cook over medium heat until transparent. Add ground beef. Cook until lightly browned and crumbly. Soak bread in half the milk, squeeze out excess milk and mash with a fork — do not toss out squeezed milk, pour it straight back to into the remaining milk. Set milk aside. Add curry, sugar, salt, pepper, turmeric, vinegar, raisins, and chutney to the beef mixture. Stir and cook briefly. Spoon the mixture into a greased 9 x 13 baking dish, and place bay leaves on top. Bake for 50–60 minutes in preheated 350° F oven. Beat egg with remaining milk and pour over mixture approximately 25–30 minutes before end of baking time. Serve with steamed rice (traditionally yellow) and extra chutney.

MOUSSAKA

All the way from Dubai, this recipe is a favorite that has been passed down to Rebecca Spellios from her husband's Greek family.

1 large onion
2 tablespoons olive oil
2 tablespoons butter
2 pounds hamburger
1 (1 pound) can whole tomatoes
salt, pepper, oregano to taste
1 (8 ounce) can tomato sauce

1 tablespoon tomato paste
4 large eggplants
½ cup white wine (optional)
Parmesan cheese grated
breadcrumbs sprinkled on the bottom
  of the pan

BROWN onions in 2 tablespoons of oil and 2 tablespoons of butter. Add hamburger, tomatoes, salt, pepper, oregano, tomato sauce and tomato paste then cook over low heat for about 1 hour stirring frequently. Add wine in the last 15 minutes, set aside. Cut eggplants lengthwise (½ inch thick) fry in oil and butter. Drain on paper towels

White Sauce
6 eggs
4 cups milk
½ cup flour

2 tablespoons salt
2 tablespoons butter

BEAT eggs with 1 cup milk, flour, and salt. Heat remaining 3 cups of milk with 2 tablespoons of butter. Add slowly to egg mixture, beating constantly. Stir over low heat, without letting sauce boil, until the sauce is very thick. Sprinkle bread crumbs on the bottom of a 13 x 9 pan, overlap a layer of eggplant, sprinkle with layer of parmesan cheese, then a layer of meat sauce, continue until all is used, finish with eggplant.

TOP with white sauce and sprinkle with remaining Parmesan cheese. Bake in the oven at 350° for 1 hour or until brown on top.

Roast Prime Ribs of Beef with Shiitake Pan Gravy

YIELD: 10 TO 12 SERVINGS

A classic comfort food recipe from David Asa and Kim Yashek, both of Vail, Colorado . . . truly a magnificent dish!

4-rib standing rib roast (trimmed weight
   10 to 10½ pounds)
1 tablespoon minced fresh rosemary leaves
1 teaspoon salt
½ stick (¼ cup) plus 1½ tablespoons
   unsalted butter, softened
1 onion, chopped
1 green bell pepper, chopped

1 ounce dried shiitake mushrooms
2 cups hot water
¼ pound fresh mushrooms, sliced
2½ cups canned beef broth
½ cup medium-dry Sherry
4 teaspoons arrowroot, dissolved
   in 2 tablespoons cold water

LET the rib roast stand at room temperature for 1 hour. In a small bowl knead together the rosemary, the salt, and ½ stick of the butter and rub the meat with the mixture. In a roasting pan roast the meat, ribs side down, in a preheated 500°F oven for 30 minutes, reduce the heat to 350°F and roast the meat for 1¾ to 2 hours more, or until a meat thermometer inserted in a fleshy section registers to 130°F for medium-rare. After 1 hour add the onion and the bell pepper to the pan. After 1 hour of roasting, start to make the mushrooms — in a bowl let the shiitake mushrooms soak in the water for 30 minutes, squeeze out the excess liquid, and reserve the soaking liquid in bowl. Discard the stems and slice the caps thin. Strain the reserved liquid through a fine sieve into another bowl.

TRANSFER the roast to a heated platter, discarding the strings, transfer the onion and the bell pepper to paper towels to drain, and reserve them for the shiitake pan gravy. Let the roast stand for 20 to 30 minutes before carving. In a heavy skillet sauté the fresh mushrooms in the remaining 1½ tablespoons butter over moderately high heat, stirring, for 1 minute, add the shiitake mushrooms, and sauté the mixture, stirring, for 1 minute. Add the broth and the reserved mushroom liquid and boil the liquid until it is reduced to about 2½ cups. Skim all but 1 tablespoon of the fat from the pan juices in the roasting pan, add the reserved onion and bell pepper and the sherry, and sauté the mixture over moderately high heat, scraping up the brown bits, for 1 minute. Boil the sherry mixture until it is reduced by half, strain it through the fine sieve into the mushroom mixture, and bring the mixture to a boil. Stir the arrowroot mixture and add it to the gravy, stirring. Simmer the gravy, stirring, for 3 minutes, add salt and pepper to taste, and transfer the gravy to a heated sauceboat. Serve the roast with the pan gravy.

CHICKEN PIE . . . THE BEST

YIELD: 4 TO 6 SERVINGS

A Moore family favorite is shared by Elizabeth Jane Moore Whiteley of the Cannon House in Watton-at-Stone, a small village in Hertfordshire, England.

whole chicken	**1 ounce butter**
2 stalks celery	**1 ounce flour**
2 leeks	**fresh parsley**
1 onion	**5 ounces double cream**
fresh parsley, thyme and 1 bay leaf	**puff pastry top**
salt & pepper to taste	**1 beaten egg**
white wine to taste	

BOIL the whole chicken in a pan of water. Add 2 stalks of celery, 2 leeks, one onion, fresh parsley, thyme, and a bay leaf, salt; pepper and white wine then simmer for 1 hour. Strain the stock and reduce. Strip the meat from the bones and cut into chunks then place in a pie dish. Meanwhile melt 1 ounce butter and make a sauce base with 1 ounce of plain flour, add salt and pepper to taste. Add the reduced stock, a fist full of parsley and 5 ounces of double cream (you can add ham or mushrooms if so desired). Pour over the chicken, pop on a puff pastry top, glaze with egg and bake in an oven at 425° F for ten minutes then at 350° F for 20 minutes. Serve with English style roasted carrots (olive oil and honey) and new potatoes or your favorite vegetable. Yum Yum!

Hashwa

YIELD: 4 SERVINGS

A Middle Eastern/Lebanese dish which is not only incredibly delicious but incredibly easy contributed by Leila Kardouche of London.

1 large onion	2 cups long grain brown rice
2 tablespoons olive oil	3 cups water
½ pound hamburger meat	whole chicken
2 teaspoons cinnamon	fresh rosemary sprigs
1 tablespoon ground pepper	2 tablespoons butter
pinch of salt	¾ cup blanched almonds
1 teaspoon chili pepper flakes	

BROWN the onion in olive oil in a large skillet and then add the beef and continue until meat is fully cooked. Add cinnamon, ground pepper, salt, chili pepper flakes and mix this all up in the skillet. Add two cups rice and then add 3 cups water. Boil until rice is cooked through and water has been absorbed, which should take 30–35 minutes.

IN the meantime, roast a whole chicken in the oven with rosemary sprigs and butter. Fry the almonds in butter until golden/dark brown then remove them from the heat; add salt to the almonds for flavor. The rice should be done by this stage. Serve out on to a large platter; add the almonds over the top of the rice. Take chicken out of the oven and break up in to portion sizes and place on top of rice. Serve with plain yogurt and a green salad.

SLOVAKIAN TURKEY CUTLETS

YIELD: 6 SERVINGS

A staple dish in the Slovak Republic from Jana Kapitan of Liptov who now resides in Vail with her husband Stanislav.

6 turkey breasts

olive oil

salt and pepper to taste

1 teaspoon garlic salt

4 tablespoons flour

2 cups Italian style breadcrumbs

3 eggs

1 cup sour cream

1 cup Monterey Jack cheese

POUND turkey breast with a meat cleaver to a ¼-inch thickness. Make small cuts on four sides of the turkey breast — about ¼ inch cut through the breast, one on each of the four sides. Coat the cutlets with olive oil then season with salt, pepper, and garlic salt. Lay the cutlets on top of each other and place in a sealed bowl in the refrigerator for 2 hours. Place 4 tablespoons flour on a sheet of wax paper and on another sheet of wax paper pour the 2 cups of breadcrumbs. Beat eggs in a bowl and mix with sour cream and cheese. Dip cutlets in plain flour, then the egg mixture, then coat with breadcrumbs. In a non-stick skillet heat 3 tablespoons of olive oil or medium heat. Add cutlets and cook until browned on both sides and turkey is cooked through. Serve with a green salad and rice or potatoes.

CHICKEN CASELLA

YIELD: 4 SERVINGS

This recipe from Carolyn Connolly was published in the Celebration of Life cookbook . . . named after a Tuscan Villa where good times were shared with special friends.

1 jar pesto

1 package crumbled feta cheese

¾ jar julienned sundried tomatoes

1 medium red onion, coarsely chopped

2 tablespoons spicy Italian seasoning
   (oregano, red pepper flakes, onion,
   garlic, basil)

4 to 6 boneless and skinless chicken breasts

1 can diced tomatoes

½ cup freshly grated Parmesan cheese

COMBINE pesto, feta, sundried tomatoes, onions and seasoning. Pierce the chicken breasts with a fork and spread pesto mixture over the top of the chicken breasts in a 9 x 13 Pyrex baking dish. After chicken is covered with mixture, pour diced tomatoes over the top and then cover with Parmesan cheese. Bake at 350° F for 45 minutes or until chicken is cooked through. The feta can be replaced with ricotta cheese and artichoke hearts can be added to the mixture, if desired.

GRILLED BEEF FILET WITH GORGONZOLA CRUST

YIELD: 4 SERVINGS

This recipe came from Jim Bressi of Manassas, Virginia. The recipe was actually made for him by his dear friend Mary Connolly while he was visiting Vail with his wife Karen. Jim has taught at the New England Culinary Institute.

4 (6 ounce) beef filets, bacon wrapped (bacon optional)

8 ounces Gorgonzola compound butter (recipe to follow)

8 polenta disks, sautéed (recipe to follow)

20 grilled asparagus spears (recipe to follow)

8 portions of grilled Portobello mushroom slices (recipe to follow)

8 ounces shallot Madeira wine sauce (recipe to follow)

SEVERAL elements of this dish are grilled and can be cooked all at the same time. Season and grill the beef filets until just under the doneness you love. At the same time grill the asparagus and mushrooms. When the steaks are done place a 2 ounce coin of the Gorgonzola butter on top of each steak. Remove the beef to a broiler pan and broil them until the crust is bubbling and turning darker in appearance, be careful not to let it burn. You can also reheat the Portobello mushroom slices and asparagus under the broiler.

SAUTÉ the polenta disks as described and place them in a shingle style on the dinner plates. Place the warm beef filets at the base of the polenta. Lean the asparagus spears against the beef filets and be sure all of the tips are pointing up, place the mushroom slices leaning on the asparagus spears. Ladle a generous amount of the Madeira sauce around the open surfaces on the plate and over the steaks. Garnish with a fresh herb sprig and serve with a big Cabernet or Zinfandel.

Grilled Asparagus Spears and Portobello Mushroom Slices

8 Portobello mushrooms, sliced into ½ inch pieces

20 (4 inch) medium asparagus spears, blanched

1 teaspoon salt

½ teaspoon freshly ground black pepper

½ ounce vegetable oil

COMBINE mushroom slices, asparagus spears with the salt, pepper and oil. Toss gently and place on the grill to cook for 1 minute. Keep warm until service or cool and reheat when ready.

Gorgonzola Compound Butter

16 ounces salted block butter
8 ounces Gorgonzola cheese
1 ounce Worcestershire sauce
1 ounce breadcrumbs
2 teaspoons paprika

1 teaspoon salt
½ teaspoon freshly ground black pepper
1 ounce thinly sliced spring onion
parchment paper

COMBINE all items together in a food processor, pulse a few times to incorporate ingredients but still leave chunky. Place butter mixture onto a half sheet piece of parchment paper and roll into a log 2 inches in diameter. Slice cold compound butter log in ½ inch thick slices, about 2 ounces each. Label, date and freeze for future use.

Polenta Disks

8 ounces polenta, pre-made in tube
  (Italian food section)

2 ounces butter or olive oil

SLICE polenta into disks. Heat butter or olive oil in sauté pan and brown disks for 2 minutes on each side. Keep warm until service.

Shallot Madeira Wine Sauce

1 ounce salted block butter
6 ounces shallots, cut in half and roasted
6 ounces Madeira wine

16 ounces demi-glace or good beef gravy
  (store bought)

HEAT butter in saucepan, add shallots cook for 1 minute. Deglaze with Madeira wine, lower heat and reduce wine volume by half. Add demi-glace or gravy and cook for an additional 5 minutes. Keep warm until service, freeze remainder.

GRILLED PORK TENDERLOIN

YIELD: 6 SERVINGS

A family favorite recipe, which has been served at many holiday meals and special gatherings from Susan Turner of Creve Coeur, Missouri.

2 pork tenderloins	2 tablespoons Dijon mustard
1 cup soy sauce	¼ cup balsamic vinegar
1 small red onion, grated	1 teaspoon black pepper
½ teaspoon minced garlic	¾ cup granulated sugar

PIERCE pork tenderloins with a fork and place in a rectangular baking dish. Mix all other ingredients in a bowl and then pour over the tenderloins. Refrigerate meat for 5 to 6 hours, turning once. Cook tenderloins on a grill for approximately 20 minutes, turning every 5 minutes. Place marinade in a saucepot over high heat and bring to a boil. Sauce should reduce to a gravy consistency. Slice pork in 1-inch pieces and place 4 pieces in a fan on the plate. Drizzle gravy over the pork.

GLOGG

This mulled wine recipe is traditionally Danish . . . and is quite fun for an après-ski drink for the lucky people who live in Vail . . . from Julia Van Lopik of Søborg, Denmark.

3 cups red wine

1½ cup port

1 cup aquavit

8 whole cardamom capsules

12 whole cloves

1 cinnamon stick, broken in pieces

skin of one orange, cut into long strips

1½ ounces slivered almonds

3½ ounces raisins

PUT all of the liquid ingredients and spices into a pot and heat them slowly. Be careful not to let the mixture come to a boil at any time. Take the pot from the heat and let it steep at least 20 minutes. Add the almonds and raisins then warm up again without reaching the boiling point. Serves four people. Serve Glogg in clear glasses with a long spoon, along with spice cookies or gingersnaps.

Index

veal, crispy shank with roasted vegetables on cannellini beans, 32–33

vegetables *see* side dishes or *specific vegetable*

venison, loin with caramelized onion ratatouille, sundried tomato demi-glace, and Gorgonzola gratinée, 66–67

vichyssoise, blue cheese, 73

yellowtail, coconut, and gulf shrimp ceviche, 11

Photo Credits

Front cover (*clockwise from top right*):
- Piney Ridge Venison Appetizer (Game Creek Club): Christopher Wing
- American Apple Pie with Vanilla Bean Ice Cream and Concord Grape Sauce (Larkspur Restaurant): Steven Crecelius
- Alaskan Crab Leg and Roasted Pear Salad (Chef de Maison): Carolyn Connolly
- Piney Lake: Piney River Ranch
- Crème Brulée Flambé with Grand Marnier Macerated Berries (La Tour Restaurant): Rex Keep

Back cover
First column:
- Iranian and Trout Caviars with Crème Fraîche and Chervil-Potato Blinis (Larkspur Restaurant): Steven Crecelius
- Dining Room (Larkspur Restaurant): Steven Crecelius
- Chocolate Truffles (Game Creek Club): Christopher Wing
- Wine Room: Larkspur Restaurant

Second column:
- Rocky Mountain Ruby Trout Appetizer (Game Creek Club): Christopher Wing
- Terra Bistro Dining Room: Dann Coffey
- Colorado Rack of Lamb with a Calypso Bean-Vegetable Crust Basket and Cranberry Lamb Jus (Mirabelle at Beaver Creek): Carl Lindbloom

Third column:
- Smoked Pheasant Appetizer (Game Creek Club): Christopher Wing
- Piney Lodge: Piney River Ranch

Fourth column:
- Dover Sole Meunière with Haricots Verts, Baby Creamer Potatoes, Lemon Brown Butter Sauce (La Tour Restaurant): Rex Keep

Interior: black and white
- Page 1, Foods of Vail Gourmet products: Carolyn Connolly
- Page 7, Chef Hands: Katherine Schmidt
- Page 9, Rutherford Maule: Carolyn Connolly
- Page 16, Tracey Van Curan: Carolyn Connolly
- Page 21, Christopher Wing: Christopher Wing
- Page 27, Stephen Virion: a friend of La Bottega
- Page 35, Paul D. Ferzacca: Rex Keep
- Page 43, Thomas Salamunovich: Katherine Schmidt
- Page 53: Daniel Joly: Carl Lindbloom
- Page 58: Wedding: Piney River Ranch
- Page 62: Kevin Nelson: Carolyn Connolly
- Page 69: Egg Crack: Katherine Schmidt
- Page 100: Thin "Vegetable" Spaghetti Salad with Basil Pesto Dressing and Teardrop Tomato Salsa (Terra Bistro): Tim Hebert

Interior: color inserts
- Iranian and Trout Caviars; Oven Roasted Liberty Duck; Colorado Organic Tomato Tower; American Apple Pie (Larkspur Restaurant): Steven Crecelius
- Crème Brulée Flambé; Field Green Salad (La Tour Restaurant): Rex Keep
- Colorado Rack of Lamb with a Calypso Bean-Vegetable Crust Basket and Cranberry Lamb Jus; Dover Sole Meunière; Mangos, Coconut Bavaroise with Raspberry Coulis (Mirabelle at Beaver Creek): Carl Lindbloom
- Wine Room: Larkspur Restaurant

About Peak Properties

The Possibilities are Endless . . .

Vail's premier property management firm offers the most prestigious vacation rentals available. With over 15 years experience managing Vail's luxury homes and condominiums, Peak Properties provides uncompromising service and amenities. Most of our homes feature fireplaces, hot tubs and full kitchens. We offer our clients peace of mind upon arrival and departure.

Peak Properties

Nothing is a hassle with Peak Properties. Our 50 years of combined experience in property management and hospitality operations allow our committed staff of professionals to provide our clients with superior service and the benefits of a concierge to arrange personal chefs, spa services and special occasions. Enjoy the advantages Peak Properties can offer you.